FROM THERE
TO HERE

OR ANOTHER PILGRIM'S PROGRESS

BY
IAIN McMILLAN &
JOHN BARLEYCORN

PROLOGUE

This is a collection of thoughts born out of my experience, but not for me. It is about living and dying, I cannot talk about being born, I do not remember because it was not painful for me and my mother was gracious enough not to burden me with the guilt of knowing the pain of childbirth. She did this for the simple reason that she loved me; therefore, I cannot talk about living and dying without talking about love.

How can I talk about dying when I have not yet ceased to live? Like you, I am a spiritual being having a human experience and as such have experienced death a thousand times and more. Not born again in the fashionable sense because fashion took me further away from the truth, but born and renewed from my own experience and the experience of my fellows. What is experience? Until we learn to live in the now, experience is just a collection of memories, coloured by our perceptions and emotions and we are living a lie, not really knowing who we are.

I am content in the knowledge of knowing that I am who I am and that you are who you are and thus we become us. Consider the acorn, not the most perfect acorn that you can imagine, but any acorn lying amongst hundreds under the great oak that has discarded them. It may well be that it falls to the most misshapen to grow out of its memory to become a great oak tree. The remainder exists to nourish their fellow during its struggle to be born and a whole generation of acorns has passed away, never knowing the magnificent miracle they have been part of.

So, thus are we, a single human existence as a microcosm of the macrocosm and if we do not see the acorn within the mighty oak then we are truly blind. How do we know these things? Because as we are writing/reading these words we are crying for what is lost, we are preparing to bury my darling wife who so nourished the world with her presence that the world can never be the same. It is so much richer for her being here and everywhere I look and see the goodness and richness of life I know that, like my mother, she had a hand on it. Not in it as interfering but on it as a blessing and I thank God for her being the greater part of my nourishment. So we become what life would have us be, nourished in order to nourish.

My beginning was an act of love at a point in eternity which mankind has identified with various calendars, according to where and when their beginnings were. As I was born into a western culture, the time and place of my beginning can be placed at about the end of the second or the beginning of the third month in the second year of the third decade of the second millennium. (1932!)

Although I was present and part of that act of love, I have no memory of my participation because life was preparing me for life and I had no need for memory at that point. I was totally and wholly dependent on my mother, whose securities and insecurities during that period would become part of my inheritance. When the umbilical cord was cut my dependence ceased to be total and I started to be aware. All I had was my five senses and, as they developed, I started to exercise an independence that had the capacity to destroy me.

So, here I am, having come full circle and survived the perils of total dependence, independence, interdependence and back to the safe and secure place of total dependence!

Rhoslan
North Wales
5th February 1997

CHAPTER 1

Descartes at some point in his life stated: "I think therefore I am". My take on that statement is: "I am therefore I think!"

So, what is thought and when does memory begin? Why am I starting this narrative, book or life story with a question? Is it because I am thinking about what to say and my memory is telling me that I should not be so presumptuous as to think that I have something of value to offer the world? Then reason stepped in and told me that I have the same rights as any other person on the planet to find out if I can!

So, here goes and from here you'll be at the same place that I am but fortunately for me, I am the only one who has control! My hope is that, whatever the outcome, the reader is not offended but maybe a bit more light-hearted about life.

It is said that when God made man, He was well pleased. I believe that if He had the likes of me in mind, He would not have allowed us to get beyond the slug stage! Using modern parlance and modern resources, we can morph almost anything we care to think about into what becomes our own creation. One of the best examples of this was when Michelangelo was asked about one of his statues, he replied that he saw the angel trapped in the stone and all he had to do was let her out!

But all these things pale into insignificance compared to the humble chrysalis. Who told the caterpillar when and where to wrap itself up and just wait? Questions like this can never be answered by science, yet science is making giant strides towards understanding the very nature of the universe and what it is made of.

I do not intend to get trapped into thinking that I may have the answer to the question that has eluded all the great minds over thousands of years! I don't believe living a hermit's existence in a cave thousands of feet up a mountain benefits the world in any way other than to allow the hermit to escape from the real world as it exists today. Again, I don't want to get into any arguments, I am only expressing my opinion. There are lots of addictive behaviours in the world today that allow people short term fixes to long term problems and maybe the hermit in the cave is using a longer short term solution!

Born in 1932 in a small fishing village on the south west coast of Scotland not far from where Robert Burns was born, spent my formative years in a coal mining community, except for a couple of years at the beginning of the war where we lived in the Midlands of England, during which time I was witness to the bombing of Coventry and remember crawling round the inside of a Messerschmitt 109 which had been shot down! Left school at 14 (I fell into a black hole called ALGEBRA!) and commenced to leave my mark on the world! Went to sea at age 18, spent 10 years in the Royal Navy, 3 years in the submarine service and left in February 1961. After my initial training, I joined my first ship, the aircraft carrier, HMS Eagle in November 1951.

Before the Royal Review of the fleet at Spithead, we spent a week's courtesy visit off Brighton. We arrived there on the Saturday and I met the girl who was to become my wife, I proposed on the Wednesday and we were together for forty-two and a half years! More about that later! I left the Royal Navy with a medical discharge in February 1961.

I joined the Merchant Navy in June of the same year (where I finally managed to crawl out of the black hole while studying electrical engineering at South Shields Marine College, getting a distinction in mathematics!) and left the sea for good in 1974.

Last employment was as a hospital engineer in Glasgow, retiring on health grounds in 1985. Spent 15 years in North Wales living in Snowdonia National Park going up and down my favourite mountain, Snowdon. Have trekked all over Scotland and North Wales, the Himalayas and the Namib Desert in Africa. I've been around the world 5 times and if any marks I left were on you, please accept my sincere apologies!

It is said that the first six weeks of a baby's life is the busiest mental activity in their whole lifetime. This is because it is using all of its five senses to collect and process information, storing it on a hard drive called the subconscious! Is it any surprise then, when we have that Deja-vu moment, we have great difficulty trying to understand why! I have no idea at what age my first memory was planted in my consciousness and I am surprised that it is still there!

The first memory I remember is looking out of an upstairs window at what I now know to be 23, Agnew Crescent, Stranraer onto an uninterrupted view of the harbour and ferry terminal. At that time, it could only have been a collage of images because I hadn't the experience to identify grass and sky and sea and ships etc. I can't remember any emotions from that memory but there must have been some sense of curiosity or just a sense of acceptance of what is.

Undoubtedly there would have been that sense of wonder, finding ourselves in this strange new world, after being thrown out of that other life where we didn't have to think or do, just be!

That is the only memory I have of Stranraer and, as there is no one left to ask, I have no idea how much time till my next memory of where we lived. It was certainly before my second birthday because I was the second of seven children and in the beginning there was only my sister who was eleven months older and myself. The difference about this memory was there are feelings associated with it, I can remember what it smelled like. The comfort of the gaslight and the open range with the kettle hanging from a hook over a coal fire and to the side, a black-leaded oven.

Opposite the range was a recessed bed behind a pair of curtains which were kept drawn during the day. A door led through to the other half of what was known as a room and kitchen which contained another built in bed and some furniture. My memory of this room was where I slept so the only memory of here was drinking some blackcurrant juice that my mother had made from black-currant jam, our vitamin C!

It was in this house where I first experienced that strong sense of security that, unfortunately, is very hard to hold onto when we step into the outside world. All I remember is being held by my dad who had a beautiful singing voice which was inherited by my sister but missed me by a mile. This is where my memory first played a trick on me! Up until the present, I was convinced that the song he was singing was: "The little drummer boy". Thinking about it, I wondered how a babe in arms could remember a song he heard in 1933 that wasn't written until 1941! A mystery that was not a mystery until I thought to research the song's history today!

This memory still has the surroundings of that room at ground level and my dad's parents lived above us, I believe my grandfather, who was a miner, owned the property which adjoined a former grain store, with the result that there were quite a few rats still around. To get to my granny's house we had to go up a flight of stairs, navigating past the toilet on the first landing!

Officially this was known as Waterside Place but we never knew it as anything other than "Doon the Lawn". The official name came from the fact that the building backed on to the River Glaisnock which regularly invaded the basement, where the copper wash boiler and huge mangle lived. This happened because there was no glass in

8

the window and I often wonder why they never replaced the glass.

Although I was told I was quite a sickly child, the picture of me in my mother's arms does not give that impression! The reality is that I had to have an operation for a double hernia before I had a memory and I would never have found out, except for the two small scars either side of my groin.

It was also during this time that I experienced the selfish side of my nature for the first time. I can place the event quite accurately in retrospect, I would be just about two and a half years old. I know this because my brother was about six months old and I was two years older than him. What I remember is my mother feeding him mashed egg and butter from a cup and how I felt when he finished it! I don't recollect playing up but I do remember the resentment I held against that innocent child just for doing what nature intended him to do! The worst part of this was that I was only a child myself!

These were exciting times in the mid-thirties and yet I was only aware of my little world doon the lawn and what I experienced there. There was Eddie Veitch the butcher and McCubbin's grocers, Clark's sweetie shop where I spent many a happy time gazing into their window, just wishing! Just along from there was the labour exchange with that very famous poster of Lord Kitchener with that finger pointing directly at me and telling me that my country needed me! A truly frightening prospect because I didn't know what it wanted me for.

I was also at this time finding out that I belonged to an ever expanding extended family, what I didn't know at this time was that it was only on my father's side. It was to be quite a while before I was to get to know my mother's side and to this day there is still some mystery surrounding her background.

I know she was fostered at an early age and I grew up believing that the Cardie family in Girvan were my real family and it would be about another 10 years before I found that I had another granny! I don't remember how I found out or even how I felt and I was still too young to consider what it must have been like for her to be a part of a family that she had given up or had given her up over thirty years previously!

However, I digress! I am still in that state of childhood where all that exists is my day to day existence where my major problems are learning to tie my shoe laces and buttoning my galluses (I didn't know they were braces till much later) after being to the lavatory!

From there to here covers a span of over eight decades, each of which experienced its own part of history and each, in its own way, preparing a little four year old for life. Because, let's face it, after experiencing the independence of tying your own shoe laces and buttoning your own galluses, what can be hard about life!

It would be about this time when I saw my first drunk man, and again my reaction was just one of curiosity but the memory is still as clear today as Lord Kitchener's eyes following me with that pointing finger!

The policeman was just a man in uniform but the drunk was the person who was to become the focus of this particular memory. He had fair hair, was dressed in a dark suit with a dark shirt and a light coloured tie which the policeman had a grip on and was dragging his prisoner up Townhead Street to the jail. I was stood outside Clark's sweetie shop watching when the policeman suddenly diverted into the nearest close where the drunk was violently sick, after which they continued their journey and out of my life! Or, had I just been given a glance into my future?

It was not long after this that my father got a job in the Midlands of England as a steel erector on the site of a new power station called Hamshall, outside a village called Coleshill (I didn't travel with this information; it was to come to me after a period of living there!) I do remember the train journey down there with my mother and elder sister and Jim, my younger brother. I have since experienced numerous train journeys, but none have come close to the excitement I felt that first time on a steam train!

During my lifetime, I was to experience lots of firsts but one of the most memorable came before that train journey and that was to be my first day at school where I met my very first school teacher, called Miss Dixon, who was in charge of primary one. Thinking back to that time, I know that there were two intakes a year which meant we would only have about six months in primary before we moved to junior school where we spent four years before moving to the Qualifying Class, where our future place in society would be decided (at least that was the plan I think!)

It has just occurred to me how easy it is, when we are recalling something from memory, to digress! So I think this would be a good time to spend a few minutes on my early school days.

CHAPTER 2

My first teacher in junior school was Miss Young, an elderly lady who was always clad in Victorian clothes who had taught both my father and grandfather! It was in her class when she asked me to go into the hall and find out what time it was and I couldn't tell her that I didn't know how! I remember vividly, standing there looking at that big wag on the wall clock hoping that somebody would come along that I could ask and save me from further embarrassment, but nobody did and I think I even considered running home rather than face Miss Young! Eventually, I did go back in and confessed and being the lovely lady that she was, she said that it was all right. Even now I often think of her and Miss Dixon because they were of the generation that had lost loved ones during the war that was supposed to end all war and maybe that was the reason for their spinsterhood.

Here I must apologise for gaps in my memory as the next memory of school was in Coleshill and that is quite vague! I know we stayed in a couple of places before we got settled into a modern house at 44 Doris Road, Coleshill which was within walking distance to my father's work and generations ahead of Waterside Place! It had running hot and cold water and electricity instead of gas and a modern bathroom replaced the tin bath in front of the fire and a toilet on the landing!

I have fond memories of Coleshill which was about nine miles from Coventry and it was during our stay there that the terrible blitz on Coventry happened and during the raids we slept in a cupboard under the stairs, I remember one night standing at the front door watching a dog fight, it was like a fireworks display with all the lines of tracers and the noise. The constantly moving search lights were a display of their own, seeking out enemy aircraft and sometimes trapping one. During the day we could see the barrage balloons and in the fields behind our houses were very deep bomb craters with the odd dead sheep! This was a great place for collecting pieces of shrapnel and it was commonplace every morning to see quite a few incendiary bombs lying on the road outside our house. As far as I know there was only one house in Coleshill that received a direct hit and I remember seeing it from the bus on the way to school, it looked like it had taken the one wall down and I was looking into an upstairs bedroom, all the bedroom furniture was there even to the pictures on the wall! Even though I was on a bus and the time I had to take in what I was seeing was probably only seconds, that image is embedded in my memory to this day!

The period that I am writing about at this time is based on the memory of a 7-year-old child which is a lot different to an 80+ adult! My perception of this time has, right up to this point, added days or sometimes weeks to events that were part of that child's experience! Upon reflection, this is perfectly natural and relates perfectly to Einstein's Theory of relativity. If we are standing on the ground watching a jet aircraft at 30,000 feet, it appears to be almost at a standstill but if we were at the same level as the aircraft it is going at something like 500 or 600mph! So it is with life; if we think about time as a child and as I can't speak for every child, I didn't have time for such thoughts! I was too busy with getting on with life in the moment. The purpose of this narrative or whatever it turns out to be is to share my experience, strength and hope with whoever chooses to read it.

We are all products of our own experiences and I believe no one ever made a bad decision in life because every choice we made got us to here and, like it or not, we have nowhere else to be and again we have a choice, accept life on life's terms or spend the rest of our lives regretting what can't be undone! I can't remember who first coined the phrase: "The person who never made a mistake never made anything". Every choice we make doesn't necessarily change our lives dramatically but a few do and these seem to be the ones that we can waste a lot of time regretting that choice, so remember that you made that choice sometime in the past and it was based on the evidence available to you at that time.

Because of this discrepancy in memory perception, I had always believed that the bombing of Coventry had lasted for much longer than it had. I had to refer to historical facts to determine where I was at specific times and for how long, the three things that had helped was the bombing of Coventry, my school days and the birth of my second brother who was born on the 16th of December 1939 in Coleshill. As I had started school in Cumnock after the Christmas holidays, that would be January 1938 and the class I remember joining in Coleshill had a table with a sandpit on it, so I presume it was a primary class! That tells me that the train journey would have been sometime between the middle and end of 1938. After researching the bombing of Coventry, I discovered that it started at 2.30am on the 14th of November 1940(10 days before my 8th birthday) and continued without a break well into the 15th of November. Which means that we would have spent the best part of a year before war was declared, which brings me to the thought that if Hitler hadn't decided to bomb Coventry, I would have grown up speaking with a Brummie accent! Thus, where it is not our decisions that change the course of history, it was Hitler's decision that caused my parents to change their decision and move back to Scotland where once again we had to depend on family and we ended up sharing a house with an uncle of my dad who was widowed with an 18 year old son, who was a farm worker and spent most of his time on the farm. It must have been quite a shock to Uncle Wull's system to have a family of 6 (3 children under 10 and a baby plus their parents!)

What had appeared to be a temporary arrangement turned out to last for about 4 years. It was during this period that I realised just how talented and hardworking my mother was! She was a very skilled knitter and produced the most beautiful Fair Isle jumpers without a pattern, taught herself how to make rag rugs out of old coats and jackets and totally redecorated every room at 71 Keir Hardie Hill, Cumnock! Her method of decorating was unique and very inventive, because of the war things were hard to come by and what was available was white distemper. She would start with a white background and then with about 4 or 5 different pastel shades she would colour the white distemper with the different shades, then with strips of rolled up lace curtain, dipped in the various pastel colours she would painstakingly go round every wall in the room! The results were amazing and yet the thing I most remember her for was her character, she was such a lovely person, everybody loved her, she never gossiped and even though we lived in such close quarters, I cannot remember any time that I heard my mother and father arguing! This might be because my father was always working, He worked as a driver for a local haulage contractor and because of the war they were contracted to the American army based at Prestwick, and a lot of the time we only saw him was at weekends because he was away before we got up and we were in bed when he got home.

Occasionally I shall enter a date but only because it is relevant to something that I have just recently shared and it will also let you know how long it has taken me to get to this point! Today is Wednesday, the 3rd of May 2017 and yesterday I watched a programme on TV called "Who do you think you are?" and Martin Shaw the actor was the subject. He was looking for his grandfather who had left his wife while his father was still a child so he wanted to see if he could find out why! So, what is the relevance? Their family home was in Sheldon, a suburb of Birmingham which is the first place we lived when we moved.

During my research, I discovered that Birmingham had been bombed 77 times but not with the concentration of the Coventry blitz. Because Coleshill was only 12.5 miles from Birmingham, it is possible that I was privy to some of their raids so maybe I had seen bombings over a period of weeks and possibly it was the bombing of Birmingham that caused my parents to move back north!

My father was also a member of the A.F.S (the auxiliary fire service) and he must have attended a few fires in Birmingham, his fire axe moved with us for years afterwards, it might even be in the family somewhere to this day, I must try and find out! I am now at a point where there is a bit of a gap in my memory because I don't have a point of reference, I know that it was sometime between my 8th and 9th birthdays but I can't remember what class I went back to in junior school, the closest I can get is 1 year before joining the qualifying class as a 10-year-old and as I write I remember it was Mrs Stoddart's class which means I did have a reference point!

I had a great respect for Mrs Stoddart, she was another very kind lady and a couple of years later, at the age of 12, I was delivering her milk and morning rolls from the cooperative horse and cart and the nice thing about that was she remembered me, always a nice thing to happen, not always the case in later life! Talking about the cooperative rolls, almost 8 and a half decades later I am living in a village called Lennoxtown with a cooperative that sells morning rolls with what appears to me to be the exact same taste and look of the ones I delivered all those years ago. This to me is another lesson that has taught me and continues to do so, always bring the best of the past with you and leave the rest. I believe that what is home grown or homemade survives countless generation by sticking to Grannie's recipe! Just like Native American or Australian Aborigine, their knowledge is passed down word of mouth, so learn to listen!

It would be about this time that I got hooked on reading; my granny had bought me my 1st hardback book called "Masterman Ready" by Captain Marryat who had captained one of Nelson's ships at the battle of Trafalgar. This set me off on a journey of addictive behaviour because books became my all consuming passion, I joined the library and my 1st love was Biggles. I read every book of his but after reading Masterman Ready I became quite introverted and preferred my own company. This was a confusing time for me as at this time God was part of my life and though neither of my parents were churchgoers, they believed in individual choice, so we were sent to Sunday School every Sunday till we left school. I believe they were both spiritual people and I have been very lucky with my ancestry, I only wish that I knew more about my mother's background, she may get to tell me one day; if not, it means that I don't need to know! I enjoyed Sunday School just because there were lots of exciting stories from the bible and remember about this time I had the feeling that I was here to do God's will and felt He was a bit like Kitchener, I didn't know what for! Of course, this didn't last for long but left me with a conscience and a definite knowledge between right and wrong! It took at least another 2 decades to find out that all this Higher Power or whatever it is just wanted me to BE!

I was talking to the eldest of my 3 remaining sisters this morning and I told her the wisest thing my father told me was: "Lift your feet, they'll fa' theirsels'" and she told me of her advice from our grandfather: "Don't stand if you can sit, your legs have to last a lifetime" The mention of my grandfather brings me to a fact about his life which, if I didn't mention it, would be a disaster in my eyes! He was born in the 1890's and grew up to see a man walk on the moon and I thought the rate of change in my lifetime was phenomenal!

He started work as a miner when he was 12 years old and carried on until his seventies! He was quite a character and well known and respected in the community. He was a founding member of the Ayrshire Junior Football League in the twenties and a member of Cumnock Bowling Club. I never knew him to touch drink except for one New Year when some of his sons got him drunk and he was violently sick afterwards! He never touched drink again until he retired, when he could be found in the evenings with a couple of his cronies in the public bar of the Dumfries Arms!

He was the kind of grandfather most kids should have because he had numerous skills, including gardening, cobbling, barbering, fishing and poaching! He was also a great story teller and because he had fathered seven children, just imagine how many haircuts and shoes cobbled he got through, he had a last that fitted all sizes with all the materials required for all jobs.

It was while we were in Coleshill that they moved into a brand new council house In Emrys Avenue, named after Emrys Hughes, the son-in-law of James Keir Hardie, the founder of the labour party. I was taken with my granny to watch the unveiling of his statue, Keir Hardie, not Emrys Hughes, he was only our local MP! There was quite a crowd there so, obviously, he had a lot of followers. The next day the statue was there on its own, the difference being, it had a dog end in its mouth!

It must have been an awful shock to their system, almost as much as it was to my mum and dad moving into the house in Doris Road! I remember that every time I visited them, there would be something new to see or experience, hanging behind the door of the pantry would be a hare or pheasant or, a visit to the bathroom could have its own surprises, like a huge salmon or sea trout in the bath and the wash hand basin full of minnows for bait.

Every Friday night was a family night of music and games which had an interval from 9 o'clock till the BBC news finished so that grandpa could keep abreast of what was happening in the war. He was especially interested because he had a son in the Navy and another in the army. Nobody dared speak during this break and grandpa kept order with a walking stick that he just had to raise from the side of his chair, a lesson in discipline!

My uncle Davy, who had been a bricklayer down the mines before joining the Royal Navy in 1939, went all through the war, finishing up with the Murmansk convoys on the cruiser HMS London. He was a very quiet man and an accomplished self-taught accordionist, he had carried his accordion with him all through the war so I imagine he was a very popular member of any mess deck he was in! He was also a very skilled fly fisherman and I remember him going up to the head waters of the Clyde every Sunday on his motorbike, coming back with a bagful of brown trout!

His younger brother Bob, who had joined the army about the same time, didn't last as long, he was invalided out in less than a year and finished the war as a postman! My dad's youngest brother, Logan, was given the choice of becoming a Bevan Boy or joining the army, he chose to become a Bevan Boy and, after his training, was sent to Highhouse Pit in Auchinleck, a mile and a half from Cumnock. He worked there till he retired when the pit shut down and he was made redundant!

I might as well finish this chapter by not missing out on the rest of my dad's siblings, his other brother, Jock was also a miner but unfortunately, he was caught in a fall and finished up with a broken back. Doctors told him he wouldn't walk again but within a year I saw him fishing the River Lugar wearing a plaster body cast! He never gave in and went on to do great things with his life, like his father he was a very keen gardener and provided all the vegetable s needed to feed a host of people. He also invented the first strimmer by attaching a vacuum cleaner motor to a broomstick and attaching a piece of fishing gut to the spindle, he should have patented it! As they lived in a block of four cottage flats and no. 39 was an upper flat, he solved the problem of having no doorbell by placing a very noisy Remington electric razor in a cupboard beside the fireplace in the sitting room and connected it to a bell push outside the downstairs front door. It worked a treat!

My Aunt Jenny was the elder of the two sisters and went into service after leaving school where she must have learned all the baking and cooking skills I remember her for, especially her cakes and pastries. I only remember her as a bus conductress and latterly as the treasurer in Climie's butcher shop. Sadly, they have all gone except Anna, the one in the laundry basket with my sister Esther who sadly passed away about two years ago. I might as well tell you at this point, it was my Aunt Jenny who saved my face when I left school in December 1946. It was the worst winter in living memory and I had got a job in Spier's Bakery as a pan boy. I was 14 years old and didn't have a pair of long trousers to wear! This is where my Aunt Jenny's uniform came in handy, she gave me a pair of her slacks cut down to size.

I'll always remember that first day, especially the walk to work through all that snow, getting there and being given a long white apron that went all the way down to my feet, hiding the fact that I was wearing long trousers without a fly!

CHAPTER 3

Here I am, talking about my first job and I have just started in the qualifying class with Miss Peacock! There was still quite a lot going on outside of school but inside it had become sort of humdrum but not quite boring. I enjoyed learning and I didn't have a problem with retaining what I was being taught. I believe I was very lucky with my education, not just by the teachers I had, but also the period in history when it happened. I still talk about my 1930's iPad (a slate in a wooden frame with a pointed writing stick). There were some things about the system then that lacked compassion and foresight, like the girl who had been in every class with me in Cumnock. She was always in the same seat, at the very end of the right hand of the front row and definitely a special needs child but that phrase hadn't yet been invented, with the result that she attended school for five days a week from the age of five to fourteen, totally isolated! This memory that has stayed with me and there is a sense of guilt that I never did anything to help her, which I know now that I didn't have the capacity to do anything at that time. What I do remember is watching her and wondering what was going through her mind and feeling a bit sorry for her.

I should have felt sorry for myself because of the arrogance of presuming I was better than her! I was to get my comeuppance though because every Friday we were asked to bring in a question for a quiz that the whole class took part in.

I don't know when it was that my dad had bought a set of twelve "Books of Knowledge" but I know they were available at this time and I perused them diligently to find the most obscure questions with the result that I embarrassed myself greatly with one of my clever questions! I had been reading about Archimedes life and realised I had found the perfect question, there was nothing wrong with the way I posed the question, it was the way it sounded, instead of saying Archimedes, it came out as Archie Meeds! Even the teacher looked at me strangely when I asked: "What were Archie Meeds last words before the soldiers killed him in his bath?"

If you want to know the answer, do what I did, look it up! That was the last time I tried to be clever.

I'm not sure how the qualifying worked, whether it was based on your work over the two years or as a result of how well we did in the final exam. We were graded into six classes in the first year of secondary, or the Academy as it was known, 1A through to 1F. The academy took in pupils from all the primary schools within about a five-mile radius, with the result that I found myself in 1A with about probably 80% of strangers and a curriculum totally different to what I had been used to! I don't think the class sizes were any different to junior school but the curriculum was daunting!

Unlike junior school where we had a teacher who taught us everything, here we had a teacher for every subject and as far as I can remember, we had English, Maths, Science, Art, Latin and French. If I've missed any out I apologise, they may come to me later or maybe the list is complete. The day started at 9.00 am and finished at 4.00 pm with an hour for lunch, which meant the day was divided into six periods of about 40 minutes each. My favourite subjects were the languages which meant the other three did not get my full attention! I could have been interested in science, except for the teacher who was a bully and I believe he didn't really like children. He was a big man and one day in class, one of the girls had got hold of my ruler and wouldn't give it back, obviously my attention was on getting my ruler back when I should have been listening to teacher, he got my attention very simply by clouting me on my right ear with a hand the size of a number 8 shovel and sent me out to the corridor where there was a wash basin and was told to wash my ears out!

I still haven't forgiven or forgotten him. That old saying: "forgive them, they know not what they do." doesn't work here, he knew what he was doing and he would be about 4 times my size! As I'm thinking of this, another teacher has just popped into my head, Mr. McClure, the PE teacher who had played rugby for Scotland and I certainly didn't like him because I hated sport of any sort as I was no good at any and there was no way I could get out of participating in the gymnasium or worse still, on the rugby pitch! There were many things that happened during that first year, the one thing that had the greatest impact on me was finding myself about number 15 in the class ranking and that hurt but, like everything else in life, I got used to it.

I was now in my 12th year and puberty was starting to play a big part in my life, I wasn't sure what was happening but I was looking at girls differently and my body was starting to behave in a peculiar fashion! These things weren't talked about in the home so we just did what all the other kids had done before us, played at doctors and nurses and show me yours and I'll show you mine. These were all extracurricular and can now be glossed over; I won't talk about my first sexual experience because there was nobody else there!

Back to the classroom where things were going on as usual but I remember feeling upset by my lack of progress in mathematics but not enough to ask for help. We were always in the same classroom and the teachers would come whenever their subject was in that particular period. I liked French and Latin better than English and the Latin teacher also taught us maths

I still regret not asking him for help with algebra and the like but wisdom comes with age and I know now that regrets are a waste of time and energy and serve no other purpose than to take our mind away from the moment! It was around this time that I decided to join the Boy Scouts; I had been in the Cubs earlier but not for very long as I wasn't very good at team things. I thought the scouts might suit me better but I decided it was the competition I didn't like so that only lasted a few weeks with the result that I had no organised extracurricular activities except for those I devised on my own, like my love of nature and time spent down the glen, collecting birds eggs and playing in the River Lugar.

I think the other reason I left the scouts was the fact that we went on a weekend camping trip to Coylton, a village just over 10 miles away and the first morning at breakfast, I sat on a plate of porridge, much to the delight of the others! It wasn't that I didn't like camping, my brother Jim and a friend, Bill Watson, would sometimes take a tent, some blankets and provisions, trek about 3 or 4 miles to a spot that looked ok and as Jim was now into fishing it had to be close to the river. We had also become quite adept at tickling trout or guddling as it known locally, it was quite an art and you had to know what you were doing and the best way to do it. You would pick out a fairly large flat stone that was dry on top and long enough to lie on, then carefully lay down on it facing downstream, gently put your hand under the stone and feel about till you felt the tail of a fish, then even more gently, with your fingers tickling up its belly till you reached its gills, placed your finger and thumb into its gills and lift out your breakfast! I've lifted out trout weighing over a pound this way.

There was one time we set out with a set plan, we were going to go with our gear and provisions to a farm with a barn that we had permission to use as sleeping quarters, everything went well until we turned in and the night noises started, I think there was 5 of us that time and it wasn't long before the 2 who were sleeping on the outside were complaining. After swapping places for about an hour, we decided to leave the barn and find a place to pitch the tent on the way home, we didn't have far to go and got the tent up beside the railway track. I thought that was it until a couple of them started complaining again and wanted to go home, I decided to stay put and told them not to be stupid and just wait for morning. The next thing I knew was the tent falling around me, the only option left was for me to go with the flow and we ended up pitching the tent on our back lawn! Much to the amusement of our families. This wasn't the back lawn at 71 Keir Hardie Hill but 107 Wylie Crescent, which had been allocated to my parents around this time and was really the first real home of our own since Coleshill. This was to be our home for the next twenty years or so and where the last three girls were born, 1945, 1949 and 1952 so once again I'm at a different address but still in Cumnock!

I was still in Miss Peacock's class until the end of 1944, a year in which the war was brought a lot closer to home by the number of troops under canvas in the Wood-road and surrounding areas, there were lots of military vehicles like tanks and Bren gun carriers which left all the roads through the town torn up with caterpillar tracks. It wasn't just British troops that were there, there were Canadian, Polish and I remember being alongside the main Glasgow to the south line, seeing a train load of American soldiers heading to somewhere else to train for what was ahead of them.

We would watch them training by stretching ropes across the River Lugar to get to the other side and then back again! This was a lot different to earlier in the war when all we had was the LDV which later became the Home Guard and we would accompany them on their route marches, running alongside with shouts of encouragement! It was an exciting time and all sorts of strange things were happening in what was normally a very quiet village. Like the Italian family who had run the fish and chip shop for a couple of generations were taken away and locked up for the duration.

One day I remember up the Wood road, there were a lot of army lorries parked by the side of the river and there didn't seem to be any soldiers about. I decided to have a look inside one of them and discovered that the keys had been left in the ignition (not that I knew what the ignition or anything else about lorries was about). I remember looking at the key and wondering what would happen if I turned it, of course, I tried and to my horror, the engine sprang into life and the lorry started rolling backwards, it must have been left in reverse gear! I immediately turned the ignition off and got out to see if anyone was about and seen what had happened, there wasn't and when I looked and saw how close to the edge of the bank I'd stopped, about six inches from a drop of about six feet into the river, I got out of there fast thinking what if I'd been caught! It wasn't the military I was afraid of, it was my parents.

CHAPTER 4

Here I am in the last year at school with no idea of what the future holds and I don't even know at this time of the decision I'll make towards the end of the year that will create a massive change of direction for the rest of my life! I suppose it must have crossed my mind from time to time whether I'll leave school or stay on and try for university but I honestly can't remember what I thought but I do know what tipped the balance in favour of leaving school as early as I could.

I mentioned earlier about joining the scouts and not sticking with them but somebody had mentioned the Army Cadets who were attached to the Royal Scots Fusiliers, the Ayrshire regiment. The uniform looked much better than the scout's and their headgear was the Glengarry which made me want to join them. I felt really proud and enjoyed my time there, especially when I was fitted out with my uniform I felt like a real soldier. What I have a very strong memory of at that time is that I wanted the war to go on long enough so that I could join up and be a real soldier!

I thoroughly enjoyed my time with the cadets as the exercises and camps were more exciting than the scouts could ever compete with. We went to a camp down in the north east of England which was under canvas and run by the Durham Light Infantry with cadets from all over and not just for a weekend but a whole week! I thought that was great but there were better things ahead when they took us up the coast where we boarded a troop landing craft and headed to the tail of the bank in the Firth of Clyde, where the battleship, King George 5th was at anchor. It was quite a surprise when we pulled up alongside and we were herded up the gangway! What an experience, the sheer size of her and the armaments, with a diver's suit complete with helmet standing as though on guard on the upper deck. I was absolutely thrilled with the experience and watching the sailors going about their business, I knew instantly what I wanted to do with the rest of my life, I wanted to join the Royal Navy. I'd had the usual dreams of young boys wanting to be a fighter pilot or an engine driver but this was different and I even lost interest in the army cadets.

There was one other incident that is worth a mention while I was still at school. It was after the summer holidays and my granny was hoping to take about six of her grand-children to the Alhambra Theatre in Glasgow to see "Brigadoon". This meant I had to see the headmaster, Andrew Martin and ask his permission to leave at 3 o'clock that Friday afternoon, you can imagine my surprise when he refused and I couldn't believe that he had turned down such a simple request. I exercised my right to rebel and I left at 3 o'clock anyway and we had a wonderful time in a beautiful theatre with a very nice tea in one of Glasgow's famous tea rooms afterwards!

Of course, the consequences arrived when I had to report to the headmaster's office on the following Monday to explain why I had disobeyed his orders and I just told him that it had been worth it! When I think of all the treats that I had been given by my granny, it must have been quite difficult, with income being so sparse in those days. It was my granny who took me to see my first movie and I'll never forget it. We were sitting in the front stalls about three rows back and I remember having to crane my neck to see the screen. The movie was "The Hunchback of Notre Dame" with Charles Laughton in black and white and I still feel the fright when I think of that memory. I only have two memories when I was alone with my granny, the other time was when she took me to see Robert Wilson, a famous Scottish tenor, who was appearing at the Crichton Memorial Church Hall. She was another very special person in my life who has had a lasting impression on my life and as I mentioned somewhere earlier, I've been so lucky with my ancestry. She was also very active in the church guild with a passion for helping the war effort. I still remember the time when all the iron railings were cut down and taken away to be melted down and used for building planes and ships. The majority were never replaced and stumps are still there to be seen by the kids of today!

Talking of the kids of today, I feel very grateful for the time of my childhood when our amusement consisted of playing football, kick the can, whip and peerie(spin the top), marbles and scraps, which was mainly a girls game, all that was needed was a hardback book and a selection of cut-out paper figures. The game was to hide the paper figures between the pages of the book and the opponent had to try and find them any figure they found then changed hands. The figures had different values so the competition could be quite exciting at times. Every game had its own season and they would rotate every year and always involved at least two participants. The other thing I remember collecting was cigarette cards, as I mentioned earlier we a large contingent of Canadian soldiers who had their own brands of cigarettes with them. As write this I'm quite surprised that I remember the name: Sweet Caporal, they were very collectable because on the back of the pack were pictures of enemy planes as an aid to identification. When I mentioned earlier that I was not interested in physical sports, I quite enjoyed playing these games because they did not pose any threat of injury or pain to my body!

The only entertainment that came from outside the house at that time was the wireless and I remember having to lug two heavy accumulators down to the garage to be charged and bringing two freshly charged back to Emrys Avenue. We didn't have a wireless at this time so this was the only place where we could have access to this miracle of modern science! Very few people had a telephone, if we had to make a call, it meant travelling to the nearest red box, fortunately, at that time, there were plenty about. It was to be a few more years before television arrived but you can't miss what you've never had so there was no way that we felt deprived because all the families that lived in the area were in the same boat except for the occasional insurance man who went to work in a suit and maybe his kids went to school in a blazer! Again, while I write this, I'm reminded how lucky I've been in the places where I grew up and how much we are influenced by the communities and families around us. During a very long lifetime, there have been many moments when I have wished to be elsewhere but I've never regretted being where I lived at the time!

I don't think I was old enough to think about what my life was going to be like in the years to come, I was too busy living in the now and maybe, during the writing of this, the time will show itself, when I lost this extraordinary ability and started to let fear interfere with my thinking. Hindsight is telling me that maybe society, controlled by some invisible force, is using fear as a weapon of control. I am old enough now to know that, throughout history, about 2% of the population, whether locally or globally have been able to tell the other 98% how to live their lives and they were able to do this by having the power and money which they either stole or were given! If the world had stayed as hunter/gatherers like the Aborigines or the Native Americans had tried to do, I wonder if we would have survived. It didn't, so we only have the baronial system to blame, and we are left with the tatters of history!

Life has taught me some very painful lessons and I only wish I'd been a much faster learner but, as I mentioned in the introduction, life prepares us for life and I did learn eventually that the solution to life is so simple, it can be described in a single word: Acceptance.

Because I am trying very hard to stay chronologically correct, you'll have to read on to find out what happens and when; maybe a little spot of mystery will keep the reader interested and even I don't know how many chapters it will take. Anyway, back to where I was and it is January 1947, I've left school and started work as a pan boy in the bakery and what a shock to the system that was! There were only two bakers who were men and the rest were women who were employed to make pastries, pancakes and potato scones, each one having a different skill. My job was to scrape the pans clean after use, ready for the next batch of cakes, pies or tarts. My first job in the morning was to take a shovelful of hot coals from the fire that heated the big main oven where the bread and rolls were baked and deliver it to the domestic boiler and get it started heating the water. This meant going down about four steps to the back of the main oven, opening the door, getting the hot coals and going back up the stairs and across about six feet to where the domestic boiler was waiting with its mouth wide open to receive my delivery. After a few days, I became quite adept with my delivery and I could get most of the hot coals into its innards. Unfortunately, one morning the bakehouse cat was warming itself close to the grate and a loose piece of hot coal landed on its side with the result that it wasn't seen for about three days minus quite a lot of fur on one side! I did feel very guilty for some time after that but the cat didn't seem bothered but was nowhere to be seen when I was lighting the fire in the future.

When I said there were only two men bakers, I don't think I was fair to the women, they were bakers too and quite often the boss would show up because there was also a shop in Glaisnock Street where the produce of the bakery was sold. It was hard work and long hours, starting at six in the morning, finishing at three in the afternoon, five am on a Saturday finishing at noon. All for twenty-six shillings a week, paid on a Saturday and some of it spent on some of the produce of my week's labour as a gift for my mother! Out of what was left, I was given the princely sum of half a crown in old money! There were times when all the pans were cleaned I would be allowed to do certain chores like making the pastry cases for the scotch pies, the pastry was already made and cut into circles, all I was expected to do was place the circle of pastry on the base of the machine, pull a lever and continue till I ran out of pastry circles. I was actually quite good at this and I don't think I ever wasted one but that wasn't always the case! There was the day when I was given the job of removing a batch of empire cakes from the pans when they had cooled enough, there were six to a pan and I inadvertently dropped one which broke into too many pieces to repair. I didn't think anyone was watching so I looked for a place to hide the pieces, there was a hole in the floor of the packing room where the loaves were sliced and wrapped that looked like the ideal place. Bad choice, it would have been easier if I'd ate it, it turned out to be a drain and that particular day was exceedingly wet and also a day when the boss was on site and wanting to know why the packing room was flooded! I had no choice but to admit my guilt and I think that was the day that I started to practice humility. I think it was that incident that brings me to the present day when I tell people I was given a medal for humility but they took it off me for wearing it!

CHAPTER 5

I lasted about six months in that job following the incident with the empire cake, I decided that I wasn't cut out to be a baker and transferred my allegiance to a Miss Bruce who had a nursery/market garden on Auchinleck Road, I assumed she had inherited from her father, although I never found out. She agreed to take me on as an apprentice gardener for a sum of twenty-six shillings a week, a shilling less than the baker paid but the hours were a bit more humane, 8 till 5 Monday to Friday and half day Saturday. There was Miss Bruce herself who worked the place with John Ramsay who would probably be described as head gardener. Miss Bruce lived in a cottage on Auchinleck Road which adjoined the house that had been left by James Kier Hardie to his daughter, Nan Hardie Hughes. Although the cottage was quite small, the property extended behind the cottage back to the banks of the River Lugar and to the left of the property, the land between the church and the river. Also the whole of the frontage of the house opposite, which I suppose they would have been quite pleased to rent out as it would have been difficult to maintain. We just used it for growing flowers in season which were sold at the market every Wednesday. The reason I was taken on as an apprentice was that the previous apprentice had left to join the Royal Navy and as I was now over fourteen and a half, I was old enough to apply as a boy sailor so I decided to approach my parents and discuss it. After quite a long discussion and them knowing my determination to make this my career, they agreed and I went ahead, got the necessary forms and they both signed it and I was all set! Or so I thought till my grandpa visited, saw the forms, tore them up and threw them in the fire. I was furious but didn't say anything, I was too scared but held a bitter resentment against my dad for years for letting his dad interfere with what I believed was none of his business. That decision had an adverse effect on my behaviour for the next few years as I had made up my mind that, as soon as I was eighteen, I was going to join the Royal Navy and nobody knew but me!

I carried on with my work in the nursery and learned a lot because I liked the work and the people I worked for; especially John Ramsey, who was married with a daughter and lived on Barrhill Road, where my parents eventually ended up. He taught me some very valuable life lessons, where Miss Bruce stuck to the more practical side of things, like how to use a spade and turn a block of earth through one hundred and eighty degrees both vertically and horizontally at the same time, don't ask me to tell you, I'd have to do what she did and show you! She called it the Kirkcaldy Hoist!

We had two large greenhouses where we grew tomatoes in season and Chrysanthemums at other times. One of my jobs was to prepare the ground ready for the tomato planting, there was a concrete path about two feet wide down the centre and about six feet of soil either side. I never actually measured the length of them but I would imagine them to have been about thirty feet.

I remember one time, having mastered the Kirkcaldy Hoist, I was working my way down the left side and John tapped me on the shoulder and said: "Don't look to see how much you have to dig, look and see how much you've dug!' I've never forgotten that advice and I've lost count of how many times I've passed it on. another job I had to do, under John's supervision was to lag the pipes on the boiler that fed the heating pipes in the greenhouses, they were lagged with what John called monkey dung and consisted of powdered white asbestos and water which was mixed by hand into a paste and applied, also by hand onto the exposed pipes so that was no heat loss between the boiler and the greenhouses. The heating pipes in the greenhouses also served other purposes when the bosses decided to try growing tobacco, I tried drying the leaves on the pipes and, wrapping it in toilet paper, tried smoking it Not recommended!

Another incident that happened while the bosses were at their weekly visit to the market in Ayr. There were about eight or twelve bee hives on the nursery which produced quite a considerable amount of honey every year, they were usually quite docile but you would get the occasional angry one which would take its ire out on me if I was in the vicinity which was quite frequent and always on the same spot, the back of my neck. This particular day, one of the hives decided to swarm and I watched them and was quite relieved when it settled on an old apple tree, growing halfway down the bank to the river. I wasn't too sure what to do as I was on my own and the bosses wouldn't be back till later in the afternoon. Across the road and quite high up was a big house where the retired ironmonger lived. I knew he was a keen beekeeper but he was then in his eighties and I wasn't too sure if he would be fit to help. However, I decided to go and ask his advice and he told me to go back, get the gear out and he would join me shortly. I had just got the gear out which consisted of a square of sacking, a wicker skip and a smoke bellows as well as a couple of net head protectors when he arrived and took over. He told me to fetch a large wooden rake, he then climbed the apple tree to within close proximity to the swarm, then asked me to place the rake over the branch where the swarm was and pull it towards him. There we were with our protector headgear on, him working the bellows and smoking them into a state of relaxation that would cause them to drop onto the sacking and all I had to do was cover them with the skip when the branch broke and the whole swarm landed on my head. He shouted down to tell me to run but I barely heard him as I was out of hearing range! The strange thing was that I didn't get one sting! The other thing I liked about having the bees was every summer we took all the hives out on the moors for six weeks to get the real heather honey which was a very popular seller. It was during this time that my granny died and it hit me very hard because I thought she would always be there. She was only 56 and died after a very short illness. I have just spent the last 24 hours with her youngest daughter Anna, who lives in Prestwick, she is the only surviving member of my dad's generation so I thought I'd spend some time picking her brains about the areas I wasn't sure about. As I had arrived at the point of my granny's passing, that was one of the first things that she was able to clear up for me. What happened was that she was taken into hospital to have her gall bladder removed and they discovered that her body was riddled with cancer and she died a short time later. What a terrible way to go for such a good and beautiful lady! I remember my mother asking me why I didn't cry at the funeral service, which was held in the family home with the minister surrounded by most of the family members, I think my answer to the question was that I didn't know but, a few days later when John Ramsay asked why I had been off work, I told him I'd been at my granny's funeral and burst into tears!

The time I'd just spent with Anna was well worth it, because I got to know her a lot better and was quite impressed by her experiences. She and my sister Esther were more like sisters than aunt and niece as there were only a couple of months between them, Anna being the elder. They were both wonderful swimmers and won many trophies between them.

I was going to talk a bit more about Anna at this point but there is an election going on today that is truly testing my patience and tolerance, so the easiest way to deal with it is to vent my feeling! I've lived through four monarchs, started work before the National Insurance Act was passed and the only time I saw a united Britain was during World War Two when the cabinet was made up of MPs from all parties and we had the best brains possible working together during a major crisis, so why revert back to partisan politics when the crisis has passed? The only reason I can think of is that it is in their own interest to keep the country divided by having to take sides, instead of allowing local communities to select their own representative without any pressure from the party whip to stick to a policy designed to benefit, not the people they are supposed to represent, but an ideology that supports their way of thinking. Billy Connolly got it right when he said: "Don't vote, it'll only encourage them!" By the way, Billy's birthday is the same as mine but 10 years behind me. There we are, I feel better after venting my wrath, but one more thing before I get back to the subject in hand, I had a title for this book before I started, it was to be called "Gullible's Travels", then I discovered Billy Connolly and another eleven people had already used that title so that is why I'm left with "From There To Here"

Anyway, back to Anna and her history, we had all left school, Anna, Esther, myself and Jim, within a couple of years and were working, Esther as a shop assistant at Lipton's, myself at the nursery and Jim as an apprentice grocer at the Co-op. Because our granny, Anna's mother, had died, her dad told her that she would have to keep house for the family as our Aunt Jenny had married and left home. That was the way things were in those days and, as she said herself the other day, you didn't argue!

Back to me in the nursery, even though we were entering the second half of 1947, there were still some German prisoners of war waiting to be repatriated. Most of them were allowed out to work on the surrounding farms and, as we were considered to be a food producer, we were allocated one and over my time working there, I got to work with three of them and learned a few words of German. Two of them were pretty nice men but the other one was very arrogant and not too pleased that he hadn't won the war. I think, by the insignia on his uniform, he had been part of the SS and that explained his behaviour! Talking about him reminds me about the time I saw a train load of German prisoners being marched all the way from the train station down Glaisnock Street and out through Auchinleck to a prison camp about a mile and a half from there. This would be about late 1944 or early 1945 and they had obviously come straight from the battlefield, there were walking wounded, some had tree branches for crutches and some had no boots, just rags wrapped around their feet. There was just a handful of British soldiers guarding them and I felt so sorry for them, they didn't look any different from our soldiers who had got caught up in a war not of their making, just glad it was all over. As I am writing this, I wonder if the ones I worked with in 1947 were among them, I should have thought to ask them but it is too late now and I have a moment of regret but it is past and I've let it go as I've had to let go of all my history and move on!

CHAPTER 6

While still at the bakery, I brought up the subject with both my parents, of me joining the Royal Navy as a boy sailor and, after a fairly lengthy discussion, they were convinced that this was what I really wanted to do with the rest of my life, they agreed, whether reluctantly or not I don't know, I was just delighted to know that my dream was about to come true, only to be dashed a few days later when my grandfather visited and saw the papers of application, tore them up and threw them in the fire! I was fully expecting my dad to argue the point. He didn't, much to my disappointment. I left the job in the bakery and started work as an apprentice gardener at Bruce's Nursery in Auchinleck Road in Cumnock. It was a much healthier job and with more acceptable hours (8-5 Monday-Friday and 8-12 Saturday) for the same money. I was there for about a year or so and the lesson I learnt there that stayed with me up till the present was told to me by John Ramsay, my boss when I had the job of turning over all the ground in the greenhouses ready for the tomato planting, he said: "Don't look to see how much you've to dig, look and see how much you've dug!" A great lesson for life!

I am still trying to come to terms with my grandfather's decision to block my career in the navy but, like Anna said earlier, you didn't argue with them in those days, you just got on with it as best you could! I suppose it would be about this time that I started to run about with boys of my own age who were also working, doing various jobs like an apprentice painter and decorator, who was to play a big part in my life in later years and others who were still deciding what to do with their lives by trying various jobs as there were plenty of jobs about at that time! I was coming to the end of my employment at the nursery, but not in the way I expected. I can't remember what day of the week it was but it was the day when a tonne of coal was deposited on the pavement outside the gate, it wasn't in bags, but just a huge pile of lumps of coal of varying sizes! Miss Bruce told me to get it in and, as it was just turned 5. I told her my day finished at 5 so she could make other arrangements or words to that effect and at that point, my employment was terminated!

Luckily, a new factory had just been opened in Cumnock by a company called John Foster and Sons, who owned Black Dyke Mills in Queensbury, near Bradford in Yorkshire and my father had got the job of driver and he got me a job as a bobbin boy with the prospect of becoming an apprentice over looker in the weaving shed. My job as a bobbin boy meant that, with a pigskin skip round my neck, I went around all the spinning frames, replacing the empty bobbins with full ones, so that the spinners didn't have to stop their machine, all they had to do was thread the yarn from the new bobbins and join it to the yarn already in the machine. I became quite adept at this and could strip a machine of the spun yarn, strip the empty bobbins from the top and replace them with full ones in less than 5 minutes. Please remember that at this time, I was a very callow youth and shy with it, among a lot of young girls who could swear better than a lot of sailors I met in later life! Obviously, I took a lot of ribbing but I was a quick learner and was soon able to give as good as I got! After about six months I was moved through to the weaving shed where I was to start my apprenticeship under the guidance of a man called Owen Turner who had gone down to Yorkshire for training. There was also a couple of over lookers and an engineer who had come to Cumnock to oversee the training of the staff who, for the most part, had no idea of mill work apart for a few who had worked at the cotton mill in Catrine.

The machinery was ancient and had been removed from the parent factory where they had been belt driven and the only difference was that the drive wheel had been removed and replaced by an electric motor. Every loom was over 90 years old but was in perfect working order, which says a lot for the tradesmen of those days! I enjoyed the work and I was a quick learner, but I hadn't given up on my navy career and was just passing the time till my 18th birthday, when I didn't need my parent's consent. There were other apprentices in other departments by this time and because we were of an age, we started going out together. There was Sonny McCormack, Bert Mclue and Stewart, whose second name escapes me at the moment. Sonny was an accomplished accordion and mouth organ player. He was also a very keen cyclist as was Bert and between them, they convinced me to build a bike from pieces of old bikes that they had and we would take a trip around Dumfries and Galloway, a beautiful part of Scotland. I reluctantly agreed because my experience with cycling in the past hadn't been too successful, also I didn't have the stamina and my legs weren't as strong as theirs! All during the remainder of the war a huge sit up and beg bike had sat out behind our house in Wylie Crescent in all weathers and I remember thinking, what a waste of a perfectly good bike. As I had never owned a bike in my life, I had a dream of one day owning it. Imagine my surprise when one day the owner, who had been away in the war, asked me if I would like it. Of course, I jumped at the chance and immediately set about the restoration. This meant that practically everything had to be replaced, so I set about getting a bit at a time and it definitely became a labour of love! At last the day came when it was ready for the road and when I told my mother it was ready, she asked me to drop in some bacon to a Mrs White who lived in Herdston Place which was a continuation of Wylie Crescent but ended in a cul-de-sac with a high wire fence and a hedge behind that. Remember that I was still small for my age and the only way I could get on to the bike was to stand it against a handy lamp post, scramble up the lamppost and throw my leg over the saddle and away I went, down half of Wylie Crescent, which had a slight slope, then a fairly long flat before a rise to the start of Herdston Place. I hadn't had to use my brakes at all during this part of my great adventure, but then faced with the slope of Herdston Place and the prospect of that high fence approaching fast, now was the time to put them to the test. I pulled on both the front brakes at the same time and much to my consternation, all four brake blocks flew out, I'd put them in backwards! So, there I am with a serious dilemma, trying to brake with my foot on the front tyre and knowing that there was no way that I could get my leg over that saddle. I solved the problem by closing my eyes and waiting for the inevitable. I delivered the bacon to Mrs White after a good cry and feeling sorry for my poor bike which had a buckled front wheel and I hadn't even a scratch! I made my way home with the cross bar over my shoulder and the rear wheel rolling along behind me!

So, now you may be aware of my reluctance to set off on a cycling holiday because I didn't really trust my legs or the bike, but because I'd had expert supervision while rebuilding the bike, I trusted it more than if I'd done it myself. I don't recall the date we set off, but we did eventually make a start and headed down the A76 from Cumnock, through New Cumnock, Kirkconnel, Sanquhar, Thornhill and finally Dumfries, a journey of 44 miles from Cumnock. Our intention was to carry on and take the A75 towards the coast about Stranraer and then back up the coast towards Ayr and the back from there to Cumnock. But as Rabbie once said: "The weel laid plans o' mice and men gang aft agley". We finished up spending the week in a shed that a kindly minister let us stay in and I don't even remember whether we stayed the full week or decided to go home early. It was quite an adventure as I remember it but I know that I'd had enough and I wouldn't be doing it again! We were great pals and at one time because of

Sonny's musical talents and Bert's singing voice, my only job, for obvious reasons would be to be their agent! It came to nothing but I did hear later on that Sonny went on to have his own accordion band which didn't come as a surprise and he had quite a successful career.

It was also at this time that I met my first love, her name was Bibi and she was a spinner in the same place that I worked. We saw each other every day at work and I was besotted, we started going out together and everything was going well until she suddenly stopped talking to me and I couldn't understand why. I was devastated and spent ages trying to find out what I'd done wrong. I finally arrived at the only possible event that I could think of and that it was about this time that I took my first drink of alcohol. It was a bottle of Melrosa wine and a bottle of McEwans export and I got terribly drunk, blacked out and don't remember anything till the next morning when I woke up with a terrible sense of remorse and shame. The one thing I do remember was the feeling of ease and comfort it had given me for such a fleeting moment that I wanted more and maybe that was what Bibi had seen in me that I had missed and maybe I'd said something about her when I was drunk that she could never forgive me for. I'll never know and I just thank God that she was spared the kind of future that I would have put her through if we'd stayed together!

I was approaching my 18th birthday and it would soon be decision time, in a way, I was terrified by the thought but determined enough that I knew I would do it.

I did drink nearly every weekend but because of my family, I tried to do it when they wouldn't find out but I knew from the guilt I felt that my drinking was not normal and that is why it will intrude in this narrative for the next 21 years!

Anyway, the day of my 18th birthday arrived and the first Saturday after I took the bus to Kilmarnock, where the recruiting office was and signed up for twelve years in the Royal Navy. On the Sunday after my father had left for Queensbury (he travelled twice a week, down on a Sunday and Wednesday, back on a Tuesday and Saturday), she asked where I'd been on Saturday and I told her. All she said was: "I thought as much, just wait till your dad gets home!" My reply was that I had a medical booked for the Monday, I might not pass, therefore I might not have to tell him. The Monday came and I got the train to Dumfries, had the medical and was told that I had passed and would be advised shortly. Another 24 hours and the worst would be over, I also found out that my mate, George Rutherford, had signed up for 12 years just 2 weeks earlier. Anyway time marches on and it is Tuesday lunch time and we always went home for our dinner (we had dinner at lunch time and tea at dinner time). As you can imagine, I didn't have much of an appetite when I heard the lorry pull up outside. As soon as he entered the kitchen where we ate, my mother said without any preamble: "you'd better get him told!" and I'll never forget his reply "told what?" I had nowhere else to go so I just said "I've joined the navy" I didn't know what to expect but I do know that he was angry and I was well aware why, he had insisted all along that I finish my apprenticeship and I just couldn't see the point as there was no need for weaving over lookers in the navy.

The storm passed but it was years afterwards when he told me that he was proud of what I'd done, he'd never have gone against his father. So now I'm just waiting for my call up papers and getting quite excited but before we leave this part of my story, I feel it is important to describe the place where I first experienced that feeling that was to set me off on a journey of discovery and misery that lasted for twenty-one years, but that will have to wait till a more appropriate time.

CHAPTER 7

Here we are, my calling up papers have arrived and instructions about where to meet in Glasgow and times. I have all my travel documents, I don't remember the date, but it was either the 27th or 28th of February, 1951 and I remember Esther and Anna going with me to the old station at the top of Barrhill Road to see me off. We were told to meet at the then famous meeting place in Central Station, the Shell at about 11.00am, I think. There were about six or eight of us, all travelling to a place called Fareham in Hampshire where HMS Collingwood, the electrical school was. There we were, a bunch of young men, travelling together to a whole new way of life and not knowing whether we would ever meet again, but it so happened that four of us would end up on our first ship together, Jimpy Paterson, Jock McIlvenny, Harry McKnight and myself. What happened to the others I don't know. I think Jimpy and Jock had both been telegraph boys together in Glasgow. Out of the four of us, I was the only one not from Glasgow. The train journey from Glasgow to Euston had us all in the same compartment and was quite uneventful until an older man came in and started talking to us, we got a bit suspicious when he got out a book that turned out to be quite pornographic. I don't think it took long for us to find out what he was up to and gave him his marching orders. In hindsight, I suppose the proper thing to have done would have been to report him to the conductor. We had a good laugh about it later but I often wonder what it would have been like if I'd been on my own.

After arriving at Euston Station in London, we had to transfer to Waterloo for the train to Portsmouth, where we would be met by about another two dozen other recruits from various parts of the United Kingdom and taken by truck from Portsmouth to HMS Collingwood in Fareham

The first thing that happened was we were taken to the mess hall where we were given a meal and then shown to what was to be our residence for the next eight weeks of basic training. The next day was a bit of a blur, starting with taking the King's shilling after being given the chance to change our minds, in which case they would pay our way home. As far I remember, only two took the offer, the rest took the shilling, after which the oath was recited by all and then we were given our official numbers which started with a letter that denoted which home port we were allocated, Mine was D for Devonport as was the rest of us who had travelled from Glasgow. C was for Chatham and P was Portsmouth. It seemed a bit ironic that the farther north you were, the farther south you ended! The rest of the day went by in a bit of a blur, collecting our kit, getting our hair cut, being introduced to our guide and mentor for our basic training, a petty officer GI (gunnery instructor) who terrified the lot of us but who turned out to be our best friend! It is so long ago that I can't remember his name but he was very good at his job and at the end of our eight weeks training, he handed over a group of very fit new recruits! The training consisted mainly of square bashing, seamanship, physical education and more square bashing! One afternoon we were taken to the cinema to see the film, In Which They Serve, a terrific propaganda film and I remember how proud I felt being part of the Senior Service and to wear the uniform which, to be honest, didn't fit too well to start with, fortunately, there was a tailor available who made the necessary adjustments. During the basic training, we weren't allowed liberty but there was plenty to do and we were kept busy with things like duty watches, cleaning our quarters and kit musters. Our kit consisted of everything imaginable from clothing, bedding including a hammock which we had to learn to sling, unsling and stow away! Our mess was a large wooden hut with two rows of double bunks down either side with our lockers in between. The huts were connected at the rear by a corridor leading to the washrooms and toilets which we learned to call heads for some unknown reason! Halfway down and between the rows of bunks was a potbellied stove with its flue going up through the roof. If I remember right there were also a couple of tables and chairs. We were responsible for keeping the place clean and tidy, as well as cleaning the windows with a form of Brasso called Bluebell and newspaper. The Navy had put a whole new definition on the term clean and tidy by our reckoning, not even a speck of dust was allowed! There was also a period set aside for policing, a term used for litter picking the area surrounding our particular huts. There was a NAAFI shop where we could buy almost anything that we needed, the canteen had a bar which we frequented if we were not on duty and, even though I drank, I didn't like the taste. I would have preferred a pint of orange juice but it didn't have the required effect that alcohol had. There were a number of occasions when I got drunk, but it didn't really bother me as I was away from home and parental supervision and anyway I wasn't the only one. There was one particular night that I'd rather forget but I'd got pretty drunk, during the night I woke up in my top bunk, bursting for a pee and I decided I couldn't make it to the heads, I'd just pee out the window, unfortunately, the window was closed and the poor guy in the bottom bunk got the lot! Of course, I denied it the following morning and him insisting there was no one else to blame!

Maybe this is a good time for another digression, when I started to write this I was at home in Lennoxtown but there were too many distractions so I decided to take myself away for a week on my own and I am now in a lovely one bedroom cottage near Alness, close to the Moray Firth in northeast Scotland. This morning I visited part of my history when I went into Alness for a visit and to get a few things. The last time I was in Alness was in 1953 when I was on HMS Eagle. I was MFV's crew which meant that we were left in Invergordon while she was doing night flying exercises in the Arctic from Sunday night, coming back to anchor off Invergordon for the weekend, which meant that we were only busy at weekends, running liberty-men back and fro to the ship. We were there for six weeks so you can imagine the sort of routine we had, getting up about nine for our breakfast, up spirits about ten and the rest of the day making sure that the springs didn't get too tight when the tide went out! One night we decided to take the bus into Alness for a change of drinking places, we missed the last bus back and decided to walk back. During the walk back, we saw many dead rabbits that had been struck by cars, we picked a couple that weren't too damaged and, after skinning and gutting them, they made an excellent dinner. There were only six of us crewing the boat, including the skipper, who was a fleet air pilot and the Cox'n who was a Scot and not very good at keeping discipline, not that it mattered there anyway! There were three MFVs in total but with a crew of 2,700, you can imagine how busy we were at weekends, we probably did about a week's work in two days! There is one other incident that is worth a mention here, normally incidents like this would be ignored, but if I don't talk about these things, you wouldn't see the progression of an illness that I didn't know I had at that time. It happened one morning round about 10 when the local constable came down the boat looking for me. When I asked him what it was about, he just said that I had to come with him to the village and to get ready. I wondered why he wasn't as friendly as the previous day when we had been talking and discovered that he was from Muirkirk, a village just 11 miles from Cumnock, I was soon to find out! At that time Invergordon was just a small fishing village with one main street with a few shops and a post office. I was told on the way up from the pier where we were tied up that I had been very drunk and used the phone box which at that time was inside the post office as a toilet and that he was taking me to apologise to the postmaster! Before we entered, my coat collar was turned up and my head down as I tried to tell this man how terribly sorry I was and, as I write these words, maybe this was the very first time I used these expressions as an excuse for my behaviour over the next seventeen years, when I was asked "why do you do this" and my answer was always: "I'm sorry and I don't know". I was abjectly sorry for my behaviour and I truly didn't know why. I am by nature an eternal optimist and I always believed that things would get better and as you might have gathered from the introduction they did and then some and also one of the main reasons why I have to write this book. So I hope this little digression has whetted your appetite and you'll carry on reading!

Back to HMS Collingwood and basic training where we are about halfway through our initial training and used to the routine which is so far removed from the existence we had left behind. The discipline was quite harsh and sometimes I had the thought that it was too harsh but then, the thought of what was asked of these trainers, who had, at one time or another had been in the same place themselves and knew what was in front of us, having come through six years of war, it is hard to imagine how much we have changed in just a matter of four weeks The reason I was in Collingwood is that I had volunteered to join the electrical branch because it was the same branch that George Rutherford had joined! What a choice for some-one who had left school at 14 because he couldn't grasp the fundamentals of algebra or geometry. It was still academic as we had to go through aptitude tests that would define our abilities for whatever jobs we would end up being trained for. However, this wouldn't happen till after basic training was complete so there was no use worrying about it. I still enjoyed the square bashing and wondered why this guy from Liverpool couldn't get the hang of swinging his right arm at the same time as his left leg. It always went forward with his right leg in spite of everything the GI tried, it was very off putting and I think it was solved by always having him at the rear right-hand corner so that he influenced as few people as possible. I hope he is remembered by the rest of the class that are still alive with the same sense of gratitude that I have for knowing him!

CHAPTER 8

Basic training is over and we are no longer sprogs but nearly real sailors. We have moved to another part of the establishment where all the trainees are billeted. Maybe this would be a good time to give you a description of the layout of the place as it was at that time, it is vastly different now, Google HMS Collingwood to see how it has evolved. If you think of the place as a giant square and the main gate which was on the main road as south, as you entered the regulating office was immediately on your right, on your left was the wardroom where the officers lived and next was the entertainments area, cinema and dance hall etc. Just past the reg office was a road leading off to an area where the barber shop, tailor and shops, and then a bit of a surprise, the pigsties were around here somewhere, they were a great boon to the establishment, eating all the waste food and supplying vast amounts of bacon to generations of hungry sailors. It was ages before I was aware that the pigs were there, I found out when I happened to ask one of the kitchen staff where all the waste food in huge bins on the back of a truck were going and he told me. Anyway, back to our journey north towards the parade ground where divisions were held every morning, on the east side was a huge stone built building which was the mess hall where all meals were taken, everything done to a bugle call which, by this time we had mastered the art of recognising what each one meant, like when to get up, when to go to sleep, when to stand and salute flag and when to eat! On the south side of the parade ground were our new quarters and I can't remember what was between there and the galley to the east, possibly class rooms and workshops as they were scattered all over the establishment. There was also an area set aside for the artificer's school, these were the boys who had signed up to do a five-year apprentice ship who would end up as petty officers at the end of their training, eventually as chief EAs (chief electrical artificers). Quite possibly, any previous residents of HMS Collingwood of that time may, if there any still alive, disagree with my description of the layout and I'm open to any correction as my memory is not what it used to be but, there again, possibly neither is theirs! If by any chance, any future reader of this book recognises me as a former shipmate, please feel free to get in touch, there will be contact details at the end of the book, which at this rate could be a long time coming or not! These last few days, where I've been able to focus my time, if I can get the same focus when I get home, it could be complete before August. I think I've just set myself a target!

Back to the training and I passed the aptitude test so if I complete the course satisfactorily, I'll pass out as an electrical mechanic 2nd class. The course will last approximately six months, with a break of two weeks for annual leave. What I must mention at this time before I forget again, the rate of pay for junior rates was 7 shillings (old money) a day which totalled £2, 9s 0d a week out of which I had to make an allowance of £4 a month to my mother, which was about half my salary! Anyway, you could do quite a lot on £1 a week in those days. The other very necessary expense was an account with the Naval Tailor. As we were now allowed liberty, it wouldn't do to be seen ashore with our No 2 blue serge suit so a visit to the tailor to get fitted out with our No1 or Tiddly suit with gold badges. At this time we only qualified to have one badge on our right sleeve, which identified our branch which consisted of four lightning shafts pointing to the four corners of a square with the letter L in the centre. As we had only started the course, we just had the bare badge with no stars attached, As we advanced through the different stages a star would be, first above the letter L then another added underneath to denote a leading rate (equivalent to a corporal in the army), removal of the top star and replaced by a crown denoted Petty Officer Rate (equivalent to sergeant) when you would discard the bell bottoms and wear the blue suit and peaked cap.

We still hadn't experienced our first run ashore (a funny expression from a stone ship!) and were getting quite excited about it, we decide on Portsmouth for our first experience, which meant a bus trip from Fareham to the Gosport ferry which took us over to Portsmouth and a bustling population which was a bit daunting, after being out of touch for over two months. What for me was most strange was the number of sailors about, which was not strange at all as the harbour was full of warships and there were loads of training establishments about. There were either two or three of us together on that first run ashore and we had quite a lot to be embarrassed about because we were so used to saluting officers on the base, it was a different story here with so many people about and a host of uniforms. At one point we found ourselves saluting a couple of bus conductors simply because they were sporting large cap badges. I 'm willing to bet that got them a few pints in their local! I went ashore fairly regularly during the course when I didn't have duty watch and I wasn't broke. They were fairly quiet and no trouble as my favourite pastime was still dancing and I'd maybe have a couple of pints and then make my way down to Southsea to my favourite dance hall and then back on board. Our everyday routine now has a sense of why we joined because we are now in the process of being taught the rudiments of our craft where we start off with the most fundamental of all trades, learning how to use the tools. The first task we are given is to take an oblong piece of steel, roughly 1/4 inch thick, shape it so that one end is rounded and the both sides are tapered, so we end up with a cone shape, all this done with various grades of files so that we end up with a piece of steel with edges, measured with a set square, if there is any light showing, we are kept at it until we get it right.

When the instructor is satisfied, we move on to the next stage which is drilling holes and then tapping out various thread sizes. It is now obvious that what we are making is a gauge for measuring hole sizes for the different sets of screw and threaded holes to determine the thread size for the job in hand. Because of my 2 years as an apprentice, I had experience of using the tools but I still found it hard to attain the standard required by the instructors. However, I did well enough in the workshops to get a pass and then it was into the classroom where we were taught all about Ohm's Law, magnetism, capacitance, inductance and how to use the various instruments for measuring these invisible substances. I managed fairly well with this part until we were introduced to an officer who happened to be a theoretical physicist. Up until this point, our instructors had been either PO electricians or chief electricians. This guy was something else again, there were two huge blackboards, covering the whole wall behind him. He started off up in the right-hand corner of the board on the left, with chalk in hand and proceeded to make marks on the board, what it looked like to me was a series of numbers, letters and symbols, an equal sign, then what looked exactly the same series of numbers, letters and symbols! Underneath he wrote two words: "Please Simplify".

He then proceeded to fill the blackboard, left to right, line by line with the same gobbledegook till he got to the bottom right hand corner of the left hand board and continued over to the next board, all the time with his back to us and an occasional word here and there until he arrived at his destination, the extreme right-hand corner of the board, where at last it all made sense with the statement "X=5"!

That is one lesson I'll never forget and, whenever anyone tells me to "Keep it Simple" my response is "make it simple first." I learned a lot during my time in the navy, but I suppose I would have learned whatever career I'd chosen, because my experience has taught me not to take life too seriously and every word I am writing has the ability to distract and send me off on another digression, which is why I have to stay focussed so that this, whatever it is, doesn't appear to the reader as the rantings of a deranged mind!

The course is now finished with nothing much happening during the remainder of the time, I managed to complete the course and passed with about 60% again on account of my disinterest in maths, We are now pretty much free agents with not much to do while waiting for our draft notices. As I am a Devonport rating, that is where I'll be sent to wait for my first ship. I haven't talked about my first leave because I don't remember much about it, except for the fact that I was a bit of a celebrity for a couple of days and the usual greeting was "when are you going back?" I went to a couple of dances while I was on leave but I think by this time I was getting more interested in the drink and I found I was ready for going back early, it wasn't that Cumnock had changed, I had and my life had taken on a life of its own, I was doing what I'd wanted to do for ages and my cup was running over. After a few weeks, my draft came through, it was to HMS Defiance in Devonport which was the electrical and torpedo school there. This was the first time that I travelled with my full kit and it was quite a journey on my own. My kit consisted of a kit bag, my hammock and a newly acquired toolbox as well as my weekend case. I had to get from Portsmouth to Waterloo, across London to Paddington for the train to Plymouth North Road, a journey I was to become very familiar with over the years. I don't recall much of that journey, probably because it was such a nightmare, I've blotted it out of my memory! What I do remember is my first sight of HMS Defiance, a totally unexpected surprise, she consisted of three galleons from the Napoleonic wars,

HMS Vulcan, the first ironclad frigate in the navy which was our living quarters, HMS Inconstant and HMS Andromeda, all lashed together on the Cornish side of the River Tamar and underneath the Tamar railway bridge.

Devonport dockyard was a fascinating place, consisting of the North yard and South yard connected by a steam railway which ran under quite a few tunnels built by prisoners from the Napoleonic war. This was November 1951 and I was not long on Defiance when I was transferred to HMS Drake, the main Devonport barracks, to join HMS Eagle, an aircraft carrier which had just arrived from Harland and Wolfe in Belfast where she had been built, a skeleton crew had been sent over to stand by while the ship was accepted from the builders and sailed over to Plymouth, where she lay at anchor, just inside the breakwater of Plymouth Sound. What a day that was when the commissioning ceremony took place in the giant drill shed of HMS Drake. Around 2,000 of the crew plus the ship's marine band preparing to march down to the pierhead where a fleet of MFVs were waiting to transport us out to our new home. As we rounded the corner from the pier and caught our first sight, it was nothing till we got alongside and looked up in awe at the sheer size of her, the organisation of such an operation was a miracle of gigantic effort and skill. Our kit was hauled up first and then we had to clamber up jumping ladders and into the lower aircraft hangar, where the various regulating chiefs of the different branches were waiting for us to allocate our mess decks and jobs. He told me that I would be in 61 mess and temporarily be working in the electrical store. I was there for eight months!

CHAPTER 9

After we had got settled into our various mess decks, the remainder of the administrative details were completed like the issue of station cards, which let you know what watch you belonged to. There were 4 watches, 1st and 2nd Port and 1st and 2nd Starboard. This was a very important document and you carried it with you everywhere and it was left with the Quartermaster on the gangway when we went ashore, to be collected on our return. The next thing was to be allocated a work station which in theory would be moved every three months. As I have already mentioned, I was sent to the electrical stores and stayed there for eight months! My first task was to go round all the storerooms and stencil numbers on wooden boxes of all sizes containing spare parts to cover any emergency. After reporting to my boss who was a three badge PO, with lots of medals on his chest, he sent me to a storeroom way aft and down to 11 deck which must have been under the Quarterdeck and just above the keel. we had to find our way around by a very smart way of navigation, numbers and letters, starting from the top, 1 to 11 told you what deck you were looking for and starting from the bow, A to Z what section. There must have been some other way to define whether the place I was looking for was Port, Starboard or Midship, I did eventually find it after a lot of trial and error, then my problem was to find my way back to the main store which was on deck 5, just off the boat deck and just above my mess which meant that I didn't have far to go to work. That first day wasn't repeated when I'd got lost for half a day because I was surprised to find out how easy it was to find your way around when you had the hang of the system! The messing arrangements were so different to what I'd been used to in the past, on Defiance we'd slept in hammocks slung from hooks and getting in and out took a lot of guesswork and at nights we'd be in out at regular intervals to get rid of the cockroaches until it became less tiring to let them share, let's face it, they had been there before us!

Our mess on Eagle had all mod cons like an on suite bathroom, shared by about 40 or so sailors, with showers and a row of wash basins. The living space was created by all the personal lockers being set up as a square with their backs facing inwards and a gap for entry on the side facing the bathroom. The lockers were two deep and against their backs was the mess furniture, consisting of leather backed benches which somehow passed as sofas but not quite as comfortable, three tables and a number of chairs. In the corner, was the hammock netting where the lashed hammocks were stowed when not in use, just under the deck head was a set of hammock bars which allowed for everyone to have their own sleeping space, also a bar running the breadth of the mess to allow us a way to pull ourselves up and in and out! One deck up and for'd was a passage running the width of the ship, containing, on the after side the NAAFI shop and forward access to the heads and cafeteria which was something else, stainless steel trays, everything spotless, the chefs behind the counter, immaculate in their whites, serving meals that were edible and a choice to make your mind up, instead of them choosing for you! Our working day began at eight, after reading Daily Orders and finished at four, unless we were watch keepers, which meant 24 hours off and 24 hours on when we'd do 4 on and 4 off. We had a Tannoy system throughout the ship and at 5 o'clock every evening we'd crowd round the Tannoy to listen to Dick Barton, Special Agent. That's what we did before television! Another time the BBC had arranged to do a Worker's Playtime concert and recorded it in the lower hangar, alongside in Devonport. It was quite hilarious when the MC introduced it as being from HMS Eagle, somewhere in the Arctic Ocean where we would be when it was broadcast!

Our first trip was to Norway and what a trip that was, our first visit was to Christiansand after travelling up a fiord which was a bit frightening because it looked like we could reach out and touch the sides, it must have been a nightmare for the helmsman, taking a ship that size up such a narrow fiord but there was worse to come as our next visit was to Oslo, up an even longer fiord. The thing I remember about Oslo was the opulence of their hotels and their prices, away beyond our means! We were sitting at a table trying to decide if there was anything we could afford when a waiter arrived with a huge silver tray full of food and placed it on our table without saying anything, we looked around and, because nobody was saying anything, we just went ahead and ate it as though we had paid for it and walked out! Our next visit abroad was to the Med and the island of Malta, I remember my first sight of Grand Harbour full of British warships and buzzing with dgajsos or water taxis, either taking men ashore or returning them to their ships. Malta is a fascinating island with lots of history but its recent history must surely be the most devastating, simply because of its strategic importance during World War Two which is just seven years behind them. The effects of that conflict on the people of Malta was still apparent during our visit there. I remember watching a man coming into our mess to collect the rubbish from buckets that hung from the end of tables containing scraps of food, tea leaves and various items of rubbish all mixed together. I was horrified when I saw him search through the debris, take out a slice of bread and eat it, not bothering whether anybody was watching or not! I know we still had rationing in the UK but watching this made me realise just how lucky we were compared to many others! Because my memory keeps playing tricks, I'm not sure whether Norway or Malta was first but I find myself telling people that Malta was the first foreign port I visited, so, unless somewhere along the line tells me different, I'll stick with that story!

Going ashore in Malta for the first time was quite an experience, although we'd been told all about it from the older hands who'd been there before and heard some really tall stories! In life, we can only experience something for the first time once and the first place the sprogs had to visit was The Gut, the scene of most of the tall stories so, on our first run ashore, where did we end up? The Gut! And it was everything we had come to expect and more, the first place we visited was a place called The New Life which was through a door at street level and upstairs to the place of business. On our way upstairs we were passed by a sailor on his way down with his trousers round his ankles, bouncing his arse off every step, he didn't speak and neither did we, I suppose he was past caring at this point! When we opened the door of the establishment? We were met by a cloud of smoke and the smell of booze and bodies. We found a table, sat down and were immediately joined by a couple of girls of indeterminate age who asked us to buy them a drink. When we refused they started groping and promising all sorts of delights until we told them we weren't interested and they left us alone and went in search of somebody who was drunk enough to take them up on their offer! The rest of the night was a bit of a blur, visiting more of the taverns in the gut and getting quite drunk. The remainder of our visit was pretty much the same, not doing the tourist bit, but ashore every night I wasn't duty, drinking with my mates with no female entanglements, getting drunk was more exciting! After Malta, I was a bit disappointed to find that we were to be attached to the Home Fleet. The Korean War was still under way and I was kind of hoping to get involved! However, after hearing that some of my mess mates chums had been killed on one of our ships involved, I became less patriotic!

By now I had done my time in the stores and had a change of duty to become a switchboard watch keeper, an exciting prospect, because while on watch I would be responsible for looking after all of the ship's electrical supplies, quite a terrifying prospect, but it didn't take too long to get the hang of my duties. The switchboard was located down on 11 deck next to the damage control centre, manned by Royal Marines. The switchboard was manned by three ratings, a leading electrician's mate and two first classes which I had attained during my spell in the stores. The watches were, 8-12, 12-16.00, 1st dogwatch (16-18.00) 2nd dogwatch (18-20.00)1s watch (the dreaded middle watch oo.o1-4am) and then the morning watch (4-12.00. The dogwatches were split to allow for dinner, breakfast and lunch watch keepers got the early meal. In the switchboard, we had facilities for making tea or coffee, whichever was our preference, always with a packet of biscuits, bought from the N.A.A.F.I. shop.

The layout of the switchboard was a complete model of the ship's ring main, lit and operated by a 24v dc supply which, with the aid of miniature switches, could control all the main breakers and switchgear. Normally, the watch would pass uneventfully as we had regular duties which were pretty routine, like switching the navigation on and off at the designated times. The main supply was 240 v dc supplied from 6 diesel generators and 2 Turbo generators, always with a couple on standby. One day I was on watch in the afternoon when I got a panic call from a stoker in the generator space saying he had to shut down the generator and I had to take it offline immediately! Normally, this had to be done by the EA but the stoker couldn't wait for me to contact him, so it was up to me to spread its load across the remaining generators on line and disconnect the faulty one. I had hardly time to think but I managed to do it successfully just before I was relieved by the leading rate and when I told him what had happened, he was furious because it hadn't happened on his watch. Still, he didn't hold it against me and told me I'd done a good job as did the EA! The best thing about that experience, I learned that I could respond to an emergency without panicking. One of the other duties that I didn't mention was to test the navigation lights to make sure they were working so that any that were not could be reported to the workshop and repaired. This meant leaving the switchboard for about 20 minutes while I raced from 11 deck to the flight deck, starboard, cross to port and back to 11 deck, checking the lights on the way. Normally, this went without mishap, except for one day when somebody had closed one of the hatches, of course, I wasn't expecting to meet a closed hatch and I emerged from one hatch, swung round to race up the next ladder when my head ran into an immovable object about two and a half feet square of solid steel! I sort of slid back down the ladder and spent a bit of time wondering what had happened, it hadn't quite knocked me out but left me quite dazed but not enough to realise that I had to get back to the switchboard and safety!

CHAPTER 10

It is September 1952 and we are about to embark on Exercise Mainbrace, the largest NATO naval exercise during the cold war, with a total of 203 ships from participating countries involved, comprising:

- 10 aircraft carriers, 6 US, 3 UK, 1 Canada
- 2 battle ships 1 US 1 UK
- 6 cruisers 3 US 2 UK
- 96 escorts 40 US 31 UK 5 Canada
- 33 submarines 9US 17 UK
- 4 MTB squadrons all from the UK

The three British carriers were Eagle, Illustrious and Theseus, the battleship HMS Vanguard, the cruiser HMS Swift-sure and 31 escorts.

It was to be a historic exercise and I am proud to have taken part and there hadn't been that many ships in the Firth of Clyde for a long time, although a lot would start from their own country and rendezvous at pre-arranged points on the compass that I was not privy to. Prior to the start, we had a run ashore in Greenock, famous, like the rest of the Clyde, for its ship building skills. Unfortunately, the RN only paid its ratings once a fortnight and this was what was known as the blank week! We went ashore anyway and coming back after a fairly quiet night to get the MVF out to where Eagle was at anchor, I had to pass some American destroyers known as tin cans when I was stopped by an American sailor standing on the sea wall by the forecastle of the destroyer lying alongside. He asked if I would do him a favour by passing a bottle of Johnny Walker and to my shame, I agreed! When I said to my shame, I knew what I was going to do with it. From where we were standing, he had to go back to his gangway which was midship and back to the forecastle. I waited till he was on the gangway then legged it to where I was delighted to see my MFV just about to take off! As soon as the boat was underway, I was approached by an older 3 badge leading airman who told me I'd get in trouble if I was caught taking it on board and that he would look after it for me. I told him no, that was the way I'd got it and proceeded to drink it. I remember almost finishing it when I gave it to one of my mates, told him to see it off, took back the empty bottle and threw it over board, that's the last I remember till I was awoken in the morning by the noise of the cell door being thrown open and told that I was on commander's report! He was Commander Peter Hill-Norton who was to go on to become First Sea Lord. I remember standing in front of his desk with my cap off, when he asked the doctor who was a witness, how he'd found me the night before after he'd examined me. The doctor replied saying that he'd found me suffering from acute alcoholic poisoning, I was not yet twenty years old, for God' sake and had a long way to go because I was and still am the eternal optimist. Maybe if I'd known how long it would take to become all right I might have done something about it at the time but life is life and I was learning to live with the consequences of my behaviour so I just shrugged my shoulder and took the punishment which was a day's loss of pay and a day added to my time for the day in cells!

Knowing what I know now. I know that I was in the grip of a progressive illness and that I'd passed the point of no return, but back then, I was still convinced that I was in control of my life and in denial that my life was becoming unmanageable.

I had just passed my provisional exam for promotion to L.E.M. and in November I would be twenty and allowed to collect my tot of rum, life was good but we still had not set out on Exercise Mainbrace. We left Greenock on the 14th of September and headed north to our area of engagement which was within the Arctic Circle. I remember turning in one night and getting up the next morning to find everything covered in ice and a terrible storm raging which caused some terrible damage and took quite a few of our lifeboats and Carly floats. One of the American aircraft carriers had to turn back because her flight deck was under water! I wasn't aware of much of what was going on because of my watch keeping duties and it was too cold to venture out on deck! This was the first time I'd seen the Northern Lights and afterwards, we received a Bluenose Certificate from King Neptune himself testifying to our visit to his most Northerly realm!

Mainbrace was conducted over twelve days between September 14–25 1952, and involved nine navies: United States Navy, the British Royal Navy, French Navy, Royal Canadian Navy, Royal Danish Navy, Royal Norwegian Navy, Portuguese Navy, Royal Netherlands Navy, and Belgian Naval Force operating in the Norwegian Sea, the Barents Sea, the North Sea near the Jutland Peninsula, and the Baltic Sea. Its objective was to convince Denmark and Norway that those nations could be defended against attack from the Soviet Union. [4] The exercise featured simulated carrier air strikes against "enemy" formation attacking NATO's northern flank near Bodø, Norway, naval air attacks against aggressors near the Kiel Canal, anti-submarine and anti-ship operations, and U.S. marines landing in Denmark

Eighty thousand men, over 200 ships, and 1,000 aircraft participated in the Mainbrace. The New York Times' military reporter Hanson W. Baldwin described this NATO naval force as being the "largest and most powerful fleet that has cruised in the North Sea since World War I.*

After Mainbrace we returned to Devonport and dry dock for repairs then back to active service going round the country visiting various ports close to Fleet Air Arm bases where we would go to pick up different squadrons and their crews. One of the places we anchored off was Campbelltown. We were only there for one night and the reg office announced there would be overnight leave for bona fide natives, I decided I'd give it a go and invited my mate, Mick Ford to join me, we headed round to the reg office where we were quizzed about our relatives there and what was their address. I told them I had an aunt there and she lived on a farm just outside Campbelltown. When he asked the name of it, I immediately said Laigh Tarbeg, which was a real farm but just outside Cumnock. I must have been quite convincing because we got our run ashore and it turned out to be quite successful as there was a dance on that night and, after a couple of pints, we went there and managed to get a couple of girls to let us see them home, nothing much happened except a bit of necking then they had to go in without inviting us in with them! The problem now was where to find somewhere to sleep, we didn't have money for a hotel and that was never on the plan anyway so we reported to the local police station where they kindly offered us a cell each for the night with tea and toast for breakfast before getting the boat back to the ship. The reg. chief never asked how the family was!

We were now into December and back to Devonport to prepare for Christmas and New Year leave. Being a Scot I always opted for New Year leave as I had always loved Hogmanay as I could drink and first foot the same as everybody else was doing. The worst part of going on leave from Plymouth North Road, the train was overloaded with sailors, sleeping everywhere, on luggage racks, in the corridors and even in the guard's van! The worst part of the journey was the fact that the train stopped at Crewe at 5.00pm and there wasn't a connection to Glasgow until one o'clock in the morning, the result was eight hours without much to do except drink and that suited me fine until I woke up in the guard's van beside an old lady who was looking at me with disgust and when I asked her if she knew where Jock Thomson was, she moved to the other side of the van! I think that was the leave I got home with two shillings and eight old pennies!

1952 has been quite an eventful year, the major event being the death of King George the sixth and the accession to the throne of Queen Elizabeth the Second, which meant lots of preparation for what was to come in 1953, like the Coronation, followed by the Royal Fleet Review at Spithead which must have taken a terrific amount of organising. My time on the switchboard was about to come to an end, but I must let you know about a system of fault-finding that was quite ingenious, there were two lamps marked + and - which were wired in series so just burned at half brilliance. If any circuit on the ship went down to earth, one of the lights would burn brighter, by a series of switching the various distribution boxes, we could locate the faulty circuit breaker and it would be up to whoever was in the workshop to locate the faulty circuit and remove the fault

My job change came as a bit of a surprise, I was to become part of one of the MFVs crew, my job would be to look after the batteries used for starting the diesel engine with a stoker to look after that and a couple of seamen to look after the ropey bits and doing helmsman. My only other task was to act as hook man to standby, going alongside the ship's gangway, to throw a rope with a hook on the end round a stanchion of the gangway to secure the boat alongside.

The day of the big event happened, the Royal Fleet Review and I missed it! Because I was MFV crew we were tied up in harbour instead of lining the flight deck of HMS Eagle. The only other one out of our mess to miss was Paddy Lyons who came from Eire and said she wasn't his queen and refused to go on the flight deck. For that, he got 10 days in cells! When I said that 1952 was an eventful year, there was more to come in 1953, Hilary and Tensing scaled Everest, Roger Bannister broke the 4-minute mile and I met the girl who was to become my wife!

The latter happened before the review and after the coronation when we sailed from Portsmouth to Brighton for a week's courtesy visit. We arrived on the Saturday morning and Mick Ford of the Campbelltown experience and I were ashore by the afternoon. There was an open air dance on the Central Pier where I spotted this girl with a knitted beret on her head, asked her to dance and when she agreed, became completely shy and she had to do all the talking. My answers to her questions were monosyllabic and she must have thought me a complete idiot. She told me that she was in Brighton doing her RGN training after getting her children's nursing certificate at Alder Hey children's hospital in Liverpool where she lived. She also told me that she had a younger brother in the navy who was a telegraphist and she had to help him pull his top off because they were so tight and I remember thinking why is she telling me this? I know! I can't remember whether we had another dance or not but not long afterwards, we were walking along the front when Mick said: "there's that girl you were dancing with". She was with her friend Alma who had come down with her from Liverpool and was also a nurse, we stopped to talk and I found out that her name was Sheila Mason. I think Mick and I between us had just about enough to invite them for a coffee, during which I asked her to the dance which the mayor had laid on as a civic reception for the ship's company, she agreed but we also arranged to meet the next day and we had our first date! I know I met her every day we were there and I also took her to both dances as two were held to accommodate both watches, Tuesday and Wednesday, it was on the Wednesday night that I proposed and she told me not to be silly as we hardly knew each other but I insisted and made her promise that we'd keep in touch and we did. She came down to Portsmouth for the review and we met again there. We kept in touch by letter and my next leave I travelled to Liverpool with her to meet her parents and from there I took her to Cumnock to meet mine. I don't think her mother was too impressed because Sheila told me afterwards that her first words were: "isn't he skinny?" I also met her brother, Don who I already knew to be in the navy, because that was one of the first things Sheila had told me to try and get a conversation going! He was only in for seven years and ended up having a very successful career in the police, ending up as a chief detective superintendent! Her dad was a civil servant and always very smart, always dressed in a three piece suit complete with trilby hat, even when he was gardening. He had been in the army during World War One and was gassed in the trenches but kept himself very fit.

CHAPTER 11

So, back to where we left off, Sheila and I kept in touch by letter and I tried to get back to Brighton as often as I could. It was shortly after this that I got a job change, Left the cushy job in the switch board and got an even cushier on as MFV's crew. An MFV was a 75 ft. motor fishing vessel converted to carry passengers and our job was to follow Eagle around the country to ferry her liberty-men back and forth between ship and shore! This happened while we were still in Portsmouth after the review and our first trip was to Invergordon on the Cromarty Firth. We sailed down the channel and into the North Sea, calling in to Great Yarmouth for an overnight stay on the way north. We arrived in Invergordon and, as I have related what happened there in an earlier chapter, I don't need to repeat stories already told!

We left Invergordon after six weeks and set off on our way back to Portsmouth, Eagle went north about and through the Pent land Firth into the Atlantic, turned south into the Irish Sea and dropped anchor off Blackpool. Our journey back was much more exciting, going south to Inverness, into Loch Ness and onwards towards Fort William, operating all the locks between. It was a beautiful journey through the Great Glen and the tourists who are everywhere must have wondered why three fishing boats were flying the White Ensign! We entered the Atlantic via Loch Lochy at Fort William and headed south into the Irish Sea where, for the first time, I was violently sick. I had experienced a slight queasiness the first time I'd sailed round land's end, which is notorious, but this was the worst I had ever felt! I remember it was quite a bright day but the sea was very rough, I was seated on the stern, trying to eat a bowl of pot mess (stew) when I had to give it up and I threw everything, bowl, stew and cutlery as well as the contents of my stomach overboard and went to my bunk. It calmed down eventually and we arrived in Fleetwood, about seven miles from where Eagle was anchored. To get the liberty-men ashore was quite an ordeal for the men who wanted to get ashore. We left Fleetwood, went alongside Eagle, took on board the liberty-men and set off. Because the central pier didn't have the facilities to allow us to get alongside, a couple of pinnaces were sent out to where we would wait for them, then make the transfer which was fraught with danger as the sea was quite rough and, strangely, we usually made it without incident except for one time, a sailor with an expensive camera, decided it would be safer if he threw it to his mate, who was already on the pinnace. As the camera left his hand, the pinnace slipped down into a swell and the camera went sailing overhead and into the Irish Sea! Because we were tied up in Fleetwood, we didn't get a chance to see Blackpool until Eagle had left. We were told that we could leave a day after her to allow a visit to Blackpool and I hated it! I never liked it since and I don't know why, maybe it was all the noise and people and funfairs, I'd loved them as a kid but there was something about them now that I couldn't stand! When we got back to Devonport, our home port, it was time for me to leave as I was scheduled for the LEM's course which I was lucky enough to do it aboard Defiance as it was also an electrical school, I liked Devonport better than Portsmouth but I must mention that the first time I saw it was when I left Collingwood, and all the wartime bomb damage was still very much apparent and it would take years to restore! My mate, Mick Ford fell foul of this damage when he was on his way to Plymouth Hoe after a few drinks when he was caught short and decided to use a bomb site to relieve himself. The problem was that, when he stepped through the front door, he finished up in the basement because there was no floor and he stepped into space. Fortunately, he didn't suffer any serious damage and we all had a good laugh afterwards!

HMS Defiance was made up of a motley crew, some in transit, awaiting draft, some, like myself, in school every day, Monday to Friday and a host of others who were ship's crew and whose job it was to keep the ship clean and almost respectable.

There was a commissioned gunner whose job it was to make sure everyone knew what their job was and after you got to know him, you knew the answer to all of his questions, even if it was something like: "what are you doing smoking?" and the answer that always seemed to satisfy him was: "Yes sir". There was also one of the ship's company who was married and was living ashore, known as RA, the authorities kindly allowed people who were RA, the duty of shore patrol. This guy had found a unique way of circumventing the system, by getting one of the other duty shore patrol to take his belt and gaiters back on board, after the watch finished at midnight and he'd go home to his wife, not coming back on board until his next duty to pick up his belt and gaiters. I believe he'd actually got himself another job ashore to supplement his pay. As far as I know, he never got caught.

Another thing I saw there for the first time was The Dance of the Flaming Arsehole, which I believe had been a tradition in the navy for generations! It consisted of a three badge man, (very important) drunk enough to be persuaded to participate. There was a snooker table which lent itself as a stage where the main actor, in full uniform would start to dance, accompanying himself with a song entitled "This old hat of mine, has seen some f'ing time" the hat would then be discarded, followed by the rest of his uniform until he was buck naked. Then the fun started, the youngest rating was then roped in to get a copy of the News of the World, which always seemed to be handy, roll it up and then stick it where the sun never shines and set it alight and that is when the dance really starts!

would have happily played there all day! The remainder of the course consisted of getting to know every part of the submarine and what job everything did. This was a very important part of our education as it was before the days of high tech stuff that is the norm today with a lot of self-diagnosing equipment. What I've learned over the years is that, if you want to find what is wrong you have to know how it works! What I remember most of the last week of the course was that I was terribly constipated for the whole week and I thought it might interfere with the wedding but I managed to get it sorted Friday afternoon, much to my relief! Brian May, who was a mate on the course with me, had agreed to be my best man and we decided to have a stag night with just the two of us as I didn't want to get too drunk, but again the weel laid plans did their magic and I ended up skint and how to find an excuse to tell Sheila why I had no money. I finally came up with a plan that she could explain to her father so that he would lend us the money for the train and ferry fare to the Isle of Wight, where we were to spend our honeymoon.

I told her that my post office savings book had been stolen and that set a pattern of lying which had to become a habit, every time I was in trouble, I always had to find someone or something to blame for my behaviour. I really felt terrible and I was abjectly sorry for my behaviour but the plan worked and I could breathe easily again, we had the fares but I still remember how I felt, standing there in St. Anne's Church in Brighton waiting for Sheila to come down the aisle and thinking: "I shouldn't be doing this to this beautiful girl who I love dearly." If I'd had the courage, I might have just left, but life being life; it has always been our destiny to spend all those years together. I didn't get away scot free though, that Saturday in the digs where we were spending our honeymoon, I was running a temperature of 104 degrees and Sheila, God bless her spent the week, nursing me! After our honeymoon, I reported back to Dolphin on the Monday, only to find that I'd been drafted to the 3rd submarine squadron which was based in Rothesay in the Firth of Clyde, couldn't get much further away from Brighton, I suspect the Gods were punishing me for lying to Sheila, let's face it I deserved to be punished!

Again a punishing journey north with a full kit, train from Portsmouth to Waterloo, underground to Euston, Euston to Glasgow Central, from there to Wemyss Bay then a ferry to the Isle of Bute and Rothesay, where the depot ship HMS Montclare was waiting. During my first three weeks there, I was on three T boats, Taciturn, Turpin and finally the one that I did my part three on, Thule. She had a number of boffins aboard, looking after some highly technical equipment to do with asdics. She was a terrible sea boat and nearly everyone on board was sea sick at some time. The only exciting thing that happened, apart from the one I was involved in, was when the boffins hung a cable with a mike attached over the sailor's mess at tot time and recorded the conversation! I wish they had made a lot of copies and gave everyone a copy, I think the skipper took the only copy! Much to my everlasting shame, I was the centre of the other cause of concern. It was the 24th of November, my 22nd birthday, which I was determined to keep secret, even at tot time because I was afraid of what might happen. A crowd of us went ashore to the only hotel in the village at the head of Loch Goil where the boffins were carrying out sound tests, A cold November night and a warm lounge with a roaring fire in the hearth, what more could you ask for? Everything was going alright until a couple of strangers walked in and I recognised the lorry they were driving. It was from a company in Kilmarnock, just 15 miles from Cumnock where I lived, so we got talking and the next thing I know, everybody knew it was my birthday and I was getting drink from everywhere! What I'd hoped to avoid had happened and I woke up about 9 o'clock the next morning in a bunk in a bunkhouse, not unlike the one we had during basic training.

The sad thing was I was the only one there! I don't know how I found my way back to the village and I went into the hotel of the night before, but before I could ask a question, the signalman came in to collect the mail and when I saw the look of surprise on his face, I knew something was up and he said: "the skippers hopping mad, he is just about to have the loch searched for your body!" seemingly I'd been seen on the boat taking the crowd back out and never seen again, all I'd done was to follow the party, so what was all the fuss about?

CHAPTER 12

In this chapter, I am going to follow a gut feeling and jump in time to just before my 37th birthday. The reason for this is, as I've mentioned before, drink would intrude all through this narrative and that is not strictly true because I wasn't writing this history, John Barleycorn was from the time I first tasted alcohol at the age of 15!

Because of my drinking, my career at sea was terminated in January 1967. I was devastated but had to accept the fact that I had no on to blame but myself and had to find a job ashore. The only job available at that time was with the National Coal Board and I started with them in April with the prospect of around six months training, starting with a month's training in basic mining skills, followed by two months underground training, coupled with what was called Kinetic Handling, a method of how to lift heavy objects in confined spaces. After that was three months technical training on the electrical equipment used underground at the coal face and safety practices to avoid unwanted sparks coming in contact with all the coal dust about. So, here I was an electrician at the coal face, down a pit when I'd sworn for years that you'd never get me down a pit!

It was at this time that George Rutherford came back into my life, I talked about how he would play a big part in my life in an earlier chapter. He had left the navy and had got the job as plant manager at two new factories being built on a new industrial site. He offered me the job of electrical foreman and I jumped at the chance, anything to get me out of a life spent underground! It was a very good job as we started from scratch with the installation of the machinery, the installation of a main switchboard and from there to the separate machines. As there were two separate factories, one for spinning the yarn required for the carpet manufacture, our jobs were just a duplication of each other, it was only when it came to commissioning the machines that it became really interesting and I learned a lot but the drink was still a bit of a problem and George was just as bad and because of our positions, we learned how to make an extra bit of cash by maybe ordering slightly more copper than was required for the job and selling it to the scrappy! We weren't totally dishonest; we shared the proceeds among all the tradesmen involved, I was also the treasurer for the social club and the holiday fund, what a disaster that turned out to be! I kept borrowing from it and replacing it till I didn't know whether there was more than should be or less! There was a pub just at the end of the site called the Thistle which became our local where I had an account, every week on payday I'd settle my account and then start again, This went on until one Thursday, the date was the 25th of September, 1969, it started out as a pretty normal day but it ended in a quite unusual manner, the first unusual event being when I went into the pub, instead of my feet being nailed to the floor, I left after only two pints and made my way home, where Sheila was just a wee bit angry, the dinner a wee bit burnt and I was a wee bit late! When we put all these wee bits together, it gets a bit heavy and something has to be said, and Sheila said it! "Iain, why don't you do something about your drinking?" We'd been married for 15 years by this time and I wondered how many times I'd heard those words when, as if somebody had switched on a video and it was playing in my head. I was on a ship in Osaka, Japan for a refit and overhaul of the deck machinery electrics. I was the chief electrician and should have been there to supervise what was going on but my tap was stopped so I'd gone ashore to get two bottles of Hermes gin. I found what was a sort of off licence run by a little old Japanese man who seemed quite jovial so I bought my two bottles of gin and decide to stay a while and socialise! He was broad Japanese and I was broad Ayrshire, I don't know how the conversation went but I got the impression that he wasn't quite as jovial, he called a small boy who he employed as a messenger to deliver drinks to his customers via a pannier on the back of his bike and instructed him to remove the pannier, get me on the back and deliver me to where I had come from. I just had enough of a moment of clarity to remember getting off the back of the bike at the bottom of the gangway, going up the gangway to be met on the fore deck by the skipper, the chief engineer and the superintendent from the Glasgow office! I remember the super asking if I was flying yet and me answering him saying I was fine, and so I was because I had a bottle of gin in each pocket of my boiler suit. The skipper pointed his finger at me and said: "You should go to Alcoholics Anonymous!" My answer to him was," You, you little B, you're worse than me" I'd seen him drunk once on a 13 month trip but he was falling down drunk, so he must be worse than me. I then proceeded to my cabin with my precious cargo and wasn't seen for 4 days! That was the video played as a result of that question of Sheila's and I didn't say anything but picked up the telephone directory and went through to the bedroom where we had an extension phone for when I was on call. I looked up AA and there, right at the top, in upper case, block letters was AA, alcoholics anonymous and a phone number, which turned out to be in the room where the AA meetings were held. I called the number and a man's voice said: "Hello, are you having problems with alcohol?" and my immediate thought was, how does he know but the question seemed irrelevant when he said: "I haven't had a drink for nine years!" My response was: "Are you going to tell me how?" and he proceeded to t tell me his story and my immediate reaction was a terrific feeling of empathy and my thought was: "You're my kind of man and I'd love to meet you in a pub!" He told me a bit of the history of Alcoholics Anonymous and said there was a discussion meeting the next night, Friday and did I want somebody to come and see me? I said no because it was 15 miles from Ayr and I'd already made up my mind that I was going anyway, even if it was just to meet Joe Dalton who had responded to my call and definitely has to mentioned here as he became my mentor of choice, purely because of his character and personality. He was retired and had been a miner apart from serving during the war in the same regiment that I had been in as a cadet.

He was also a great Burns fan and had the same understanding of the human condition that Burns had. He was never without his notebook, full of quotes from Burns or Dylan Thomas, where he always seemed to pick one to suit the occasion! I remember getting up on the Friday morning feeling that there was something of great import taking place that day and it was only because of a decision I'd made!

There was only a decision with no action at this point and I had the rest of the day to get through before the action could take place and the frightening thing about this was I was to remember all the decisions I'd made in the past with no following action. Anyway, I made it till my shift was over and got home to prepare for the ordeal ahead. The time came, dinner over and I'm dressed to kill, face washed, in a suit, collar and tie and not smelling of booze! Then came the journey, I'd previously been convicted of drunk driving and spent two years of a three years sentence, so my 1st thought was: "I hope I get stopped by the police and breathalysed," because I wanted the world to know that it was safe! That thought did what every thought does, brings in another one and the thought that followed absolutely terrified me because, if the world was to be truly saved, I couldn't drink alcohol ever again and the thought almost made me turn the car around and head home. However, I remembered my promise to Joe and I carried on. The next thought: "what if somebody sees me and asks where I'm going?" I was getting good at this and I already had an excuse prepared. I wasn't going to tell anyone I was going to an AA meeting. If I was stopped, all I was going to say was: "I'm going down to the harbour to look at the boats". Needless to say, none of these things happened but even so, I parked at the top of the Sandgate, about 400 yards from the meeting place at number 9. I arrived at No.9 and was met by a tall man in a light coloured coat who asked me, in very posh voice: "Are you Iain?" and when I answered in the affirmative, he shook my hand warmly and said: "you're very welcome, my name's John, come upstairs and meet everybody." I must admit to a feeling of a slight apprehension, because the minute I walked into that room, I knew that my journey was over and you'll have to excuse me for a few minutes because the emotion that overtook me by reliving those moments was so powerful, that I burst into tears! I'm not going to apologise because it was a very cleansing few moments and these are the times that I can never forget. It was the feeling in that room which was so full of love, that I knew that I had found what I had set out to find all those years ago! For the first time in my living memory, I felt a sense of belonging. From a very early age, I'd felt apart from almost everything most of my life and here, at last, I felt a part of something good and it was only when the meeting proper started, it became immediately obvious the difference between here and a pub, here there would be only one person talking and everybody else listening and in a pub, everybody talking and nobody listening!

When they found out that this was my first meeting, everybody made such a fuss of me and told me to keep coming back! There were only about six of us at that meeting, 3 women and 3 men, including me, there was a Christine, a Margaret and I can't remember the other woman's but they made up the fellowship of men and women that the preamble talks about. There was John, who had met me at the door and there was Joe, who I regarded as my saviour as he'd introduced me to this fantastic programme! There were two big parchments, hanging on the wall, one containing the twelve steps and the other the twelve traditions of Alcoholics Anonymous. There was a bit of sharing going and I was told if I didn't want to say anything, I didn't have to and I honestly can't remember whether I did or not, I was too busy enjoying the moment. I got so much identification, that I thought somebody had told them about me because they were talking about me. This is where that feeling of empathy came from when I was talking to Joe, the previous night, it was also Joe who told me that very first night: "Iain, you need never drink again!." I was amazed and feeling so great that on the Saturday morning after the meeting, I told Sheila that I'd stopped drinking and I intended to die sober!

Remember, we'd been married at this time for just over 15 years, so is it any wonder that it took almost 1 year to convince her that this would be the end of her troubles! This concludes this edition of "Back to the Future" Time now for "Back to where we left off!" in Chapter 13

CHAPTER 13

Here we are now into 1955 and I have moved from Thule to Alderney, an A class submarine and much more comfortable than the Thule. All the time I've been in Rothesay, I've managed most months to get a weekend in Brighton with Sheila, which were very precious but the journey was, as explained earlier quite daunting, I'd leave Rothesay about 10 o'clock and arrive at the flat, dead on midnight! The journey back was a lot easier because I'd arrive in Euston early enough to imbibe enough rum to get me to sleep through to Glasgow! Alderney is due to leave for Halifax, Nova Scotia in the summer to make up the numbers of the brand new 6th Submarine Squadron, the other two are already out there waiting, Astute and Ambush, meanwhile the skipper, Lieutenant Commander David Teare is running us ragged with unending exercises, just so we get the drill right. There was one day I counted 18 dives on the klaxon, which meant that whatever you were doing had to be dropped and everyone went to diving stations. He was a good skipper though and everything he did had a purpose and he soon had us licked into shape. There was one time, later in the commission, when I was on watch, we were dived and going slow ahead, group down when the starboard telegraph went from group down to shafts in series, this was the first time we had ever gone into silent routine and I had to think fast! Was he testing me? I knew how to go group down, but something in my head told me that to go into group down, you only obeyed the port telegraph, Fleet Standing Orders, so I did nothing and the starboard telegraph rang again and even though I was crapping myself, I stuck to my guns and the next thing big David came storming into the motor room and demanded to know what the F——- I was doing? I quoted the Standing Order to him and all he said was: "obey the telegraph," and stormed off. It was quite some time later that I found out that when he got back to the control room, he sent the Sub to get the Standing Orders and look up the relevant subject. He found out that I was right, but never apologised to me, instead he apologised to my boss, who never passed the apology on! I never had the same respect for my boss again!

So, we are on the move again, but not by train this time, carrying all our kit, we are now being carried from Portsmouth direct to Devonport by submarine, which has all our kit on board, definitely a better way to travel! We will be there for two months in dry dock for refit and embarkation leave of a month before our trip out to Canada. It means us getting digs ashore while we are there and travelling back and forth every day, only staying on board when we are duty watch. There are differences since the last time I was here, the big one being that Defiance has disappeared from the Tamar and a lot of reconstruction has taken place, there is still a lot to be done, but they are getting there. The other thing is that rationing has stopped and we no longer need to give our ration points up when we go on leave! We still have a large fleet, although a lot of it is mothballed in the north yard, we are dry docked in the south yard in one of two docks with a laundry and toilet block in between. I don't know how long we'd been there when one of the stokers came back with a pet rhesus monkey that he had purchased from a local pet store. It wasn't long before he was given a name, Clem because he looked a lot like our then prime minister! He soon settled in and seemed quite happy, so the skipper gave us permission to keep him. He didn't trouble anybody unless he didn't recognise them and they were attempting to come aboard, then his hackles were up and teeth bared until someone came and allowed them aboard. He was alright then, but what amazed me was how quickly he came to know who was crew and who was not! He was quite a character and became somewhat famous for his antics, you wouldn't want to make an enemy of him! He soon got to know who lived where and he definitely had his favourites! Whenever he approached the engine room, it was quite normal for a wheel spanner to be thrown at him, usually by the chief ERA! Was it any surprise to them, however, to enter their mess one time to find on the mess table, a full carton of cigarettes opened and every individual packet emptied, every cigarette torn in half, a little pyramid built of the debris and the contents of the teapot made a soggy mess of the whole? Another time, we were in the wash room and had Clem with us, with the idea that we'd take the opportunity to give him a bath. There was a frigate in the adjoining dry dock and unbeknown to us, there was a petty officer from there, in one of the toilet cubicles. Clem absolutely hated water, so you can imagine how surprised this chap felt, when he had a wild monkey with bared teeth, squatting on the cistern behind his head! He didn't know that all we'd done was to try and get him in the sink!

The time soon passed, because, with everyone having a month's embarkation leave, it meant only a month in Devonport, this was the longest time Sheila and I had spent together and by this time she had managed to rent a much nicer flat from a lovely older couple, called Mr and Mrs Ogle who were very kind to us. We spent a bit of our leave with each of our parents, but most of it in Brighton, where we walked a lot on the South Downs which I remember as the happiest of times and where I spend most of my memories of my darling Sheila! Sorry, I digressed again and emotion took charge! Anyway, we are back in Portsmouth preparing for our departure and Sheila has arranged for some time off and is here for a few days before we leave, she is staying with Brian May's aunt and uncle who live in Portsmouth and were at our wedding because Brian was my best man, having done the submarine course with me. The day came when we said our goodbyes and we were off, thinking that it would be another two and a half years before we'd be together again, a daunting thought, although life has its surprises and we'd be together again much sooner than expected! The journey across the North Atlantic was fairly uneventful, except for the day when we passed the SS United States, going the other way. She had just taken the Blue Riband from our Queen Mary recently, and as I was watching her through the periscope, I thought: "what a chance to get our own back!" Good job I wasn't in charge! When we finally arrived in Halifax, I can't remember how long it took, I was in for quite a surprise. The 6th submarine squadron wasn't alongside a depot ship but quartered in HMCS Stadacona, a large Naval base that backed down to the harbour where we were tied up alongside the other two submarines that comprised the squadron, Ambush and Astute. I don't think we were relieving another boat, we were just making up the numbers of the very first 6th submarine squadron in Canada! Our quarters were in a two story wooden building, divided into four sections, two on ground level and two on the upper level. The bottom right was reserved for the spare crew and the other three for the boats when not at sea. It was then that I discovered that Don, Sheila's brother was there as spare crew. He was a leading telegraphist, working as part of Commander S/M's staff, a real cushy number and I think he only ever served on one submarine, Seraph for about six weeks in all of his submarine service! I was dead jealous of him! Another sign of the insecurities that were starting to manifest themselves in my life!

In fact, it was because Don was out there that Sheila and I were to get together sooner than expected, but it would take some time to organise! As this was a new squadron, no arrangements were in place to bring wives out and any who wanted to had to finance it themselves. I know we didn't consider it till nearly the end of the year and, in the meantime, life went on and we got to know about life in Nova Scotia! It was a dry province, which meant that to buy liquor, one had to purchase a liquor licence, which allowed you to buy the necessary from a liquor store and take it to a place of safety where it could be drunk. If one was caught with an opened bottle, he was charged with illegal possession and fined accordingly. The taverns were allowed to sell beer only and in small glasses with salt shakers that the locals put in the beer, the salt, not the shakers! I don't know why they did it but we just followed their example and got used to it! Because of these laws, it meant that there was a thriving bootlegging industry in Halifax and it didn't take long for us to find out where they were! The other things we had to get used to was the standard of living here, compared to the austerity of Britain and supermarkets which haven't appeared in Britain yet. The weather at that time, in Halifax, was very warm and lasted until late August, early September but we were in for a nasty surprise come October when the first snowfall of the year happened and didn't let up until the following May!

We didn't do too badly though, as most of our exercising was done off Bermuda in the West Indies, where at times the sea temperature was 82 degrees Fahrenheit! Every lunchtime we would surface and "Hands to Bathe" would sound and the ones not on watch would have a nice relaxing half hour in the water, with the gun-layer on watch in the conning tower with a loaded rifle, just in case of sharks. One day, someone decided to see what would happen if Clem was thrown into the water, I don't think his feet barely got wet, as soon as his feet touched the water, he leapt onto the nearest swimmer's head and would not let go! Another time, while back in Halifax, we decided to have a banyan in the country, so a crowd of us, including Clem, set off with a load of food and booze, ending up in this field, under a huge tree for shade and proceeded to have a good time, lots of singing, telling stories and not a care in the world until someone asked: "I wonder if Clem still remembers how to climb trees?" There's poor old Clem minding his own business, enjoying himself when he is grabbed and, unceremoniously pushed onto the tree and told to climb. I'm sure it was the last thing he wanted to do because he just sat there looking at us and refusing to move until a barrage of sticks and bits of food made him get as far away from us as possible, and that meant right to the top of the tree, and there he stayed and no enticement could get him to come down. I think we had got out there by bus and arranged a time for the bus to collect us. That time was approaching fast and Clem was still in a huff up a tree. I'm almost sure it was Kiwi, who had bought Clem in the first place, who volunteered to climb up and bring him down, after all, he was his best pal! The only problem with this was that Kiwi was pretty drunk and not used to climbing trees! We're all on the ground, looking up when Kiwi was just about to grab Clem when he decided to come down on his own, knocking Kiwi off balance and he came down faster than he went up! Fortunately, he was drunk enough to fall relaxed and no serious injuries were sustained! I think that was the last time that Clem was put to the test, he'd passed his part three!

October arrived and with it the snow and freezing temperatures, which meant Arctic clothing when on the casing or anywhere else outside! We had another trip to Bermuda in the meantime, which was a pleasant break from the weather in Halifax. At this time, it was quite common for me to be under stoppage of leave for something or other and it so happened that this was one of the times, the officer of the watch must have felt a bit sorry for me as he sent me ashore in charge of the shore patrol! We always exercised with a Canadian destroyer, so there were both Canadian and Royal Navy men ashore and usually they got on fine together but this particular night some of our boys must have upset one of theirs. We were standing outside the door of this dance hall when the aggrieved rating appeared and grabbed me by whatever was covering my chest and asked: "What are you going to do about it?"! He must have been the biggest rating they had and he had me by the chest, I did the only thing I could think of, I looked him in the eye and said: "If you keep quiet about this, I'll not say a word, and it'll all be forgotten". There was nobody more surprised than me when it worked and he just turned and went back into the dance!

We're now back in Halifax and it is November, we have been here almost six months and now due a week's station leave. My aunt Anna who is my dad's youngest sister is married and now living in Syracuse, New York state, so I decide to give her a call with a view to visiting them. Of course, if I'd known then that Sheila and her sister-in-law were coming out in March, I'd have saved my leave till then.

However, the trip went ahead and I travelled by coach through Nova Scotia, New Brunswick, Quebec and down through the Maritime States and changed coaches in Boston for Syracuse. Jim, Anna's husband, had done his National Service in the UK and as soon as they arrived in America or very shortly after, he was drafted into the American army! The good thing about that was, they got immediate American Citizenship and so had their children. I had a fantastic time there, but the best thing ever was being taken by Jim to this huge Sports Stadium to watch some All-In wrestling. Imagine my surprise when I found out that on the bill was Primo Carnera v Yukon Eric, it wasn't so much that I was excited about, Joe Louis, my boyhood hero was refereeing the match, that one event made the visit worth it!

CHAPTER 14

We are really into the winter here in Halifax, with temperatures well below freezing and a real requirement for the Arctic clothing we've been provided with. As Don is with Commander S/M's staff, he's had a lot of help with organising Sylvia and Sheila's trip out to join us for the duration of our stay, which is excellent news and means that we will have to find a place to rent, but we can do that when we know the date of their arrival. I have made friends with a local family, Mom and Pop Newton who made us very welcome and we visited with them on a regular basis. Their son-in-law, John Taylor was from Southampton originally and in the RN but transferred to the Canadian Navy when he married their daughter. Pop Newton brewed and bottled his own beer in the basement which was freely sampled whenever we visited.

I can't remember whether it was a Xmas or New Year's dance that Stadacona had laid on but we attended it anyway and got talking to a couple of girls from Glasgow, who were out there on holiday. I was with our cook, a mad Irishman who was in the Canadian Navy but had volunteered for submarine service. When the girls said they were going home, he insisted that we'd see them safely home as this was a pretty wild area and ordered a taxi. I wasn't drunk and I agreed to go with them but only to deliver them to their digs! We dropped them and made our way back and, as was generally the case, we'd drop into Dalo's, a cafe opposite the main gate on Gottingen Street. As they drive on the right-hand side over there, the taxi stopped across the road from Dalo's and I could see tables, chairs and bodies flying all over the place. I said to the mad Irishman, because I was sober: "I'm not going in there, if you want a hamburger, I'll pay the taxi and wait for you,"

93

In he strolled, bold as brass and I crossed the street and stood outside waiting for him when it was almost a repeat of my Bermuda experience, a guy of about the same size, only black asked me the same question: "What are you going to do about it?" My answer was: "Do about what, I've only just got here!" A bottle appeared from somewhere and he smacked me a couple of times over the head with it and ran off. The next thing I knew there were police and medics from the base, arguing who had prior claim, luckily the medics won and I was in sick bay for a couple of days and when I was released, I had a couple of real shiners and a couple of stitched scars across my forehead! What a reward for doing a couple of Scots lassies a favour. If either of you are still alive and get to read this, please don't feel bad, blame it on the mad Irishman, he got away scot free! A few nights later, sitting in my usual bootleggers on my own, when the girl who was serving asked: "what happened to you?" and with my usual tact answered: "One of those big black bastards hit me with a bottle," and I remembered where I was and got out pretty quick! This was probably the only time I can remember getting in trouble when I was sober.

We are now into January and the snow is piling up still and drivers have their snow tyres and chains on. It is also the hunting season and the numbers of accidents that happen is ridiculous, considering all the precautions they are told to take! One guy with a station wagon left the back open with a brown blanket while he went to collect a deer he had shot when some idiot, mistaking the blanket for a deer, shot a hole in the petrol tank! Another time, I watched a pickup truck with a stag strapped across its bonnet, driving on all four wheel rims, with shreds of tyres slapping the road, he must have got caught with no spare and just decided to carry on!

We now know the arrangements are complete for our wives to come out, so we have managed to rent a detached house, 892 Robie Street, Halifax and they have booked passage on MS Scythia, a Cunard passenger carrying cargo ship, arriving about the middle of March. It looks like I will be in Halifax when they arrive so that I will be here to meet them off the boat. I am feeling quite nervous and wondering if she will recognise me as I've grown a full beard and, though they won't be immediately apparent, I've had two tattoos, one on each forearm, the one on the left of a Highland lassie with the word Sheila in a scroll and on the right, a White Ensign enclosing a sinking ship, with the inscription "A sailor's grave!" I think the tattooist was more drunk than I was when he did them, today they are unreadable!

Our immediate task was to make sure that 892, Robie Street was ready for their arrival and that there were enough groceries in the larder. Unfortunately, Don died a few years ago and I am unable to consult with him about who did what, so I'm going to assume that I was responsible enough and did my fair share of the chores! The only thing that is clear in my mind around this time is meeting them as they got off the ship and catching sight of them when they had cleared immigration The emotion I felt is getting to me again as I relive the moment and the guilt I feel now that I know what is in front of this beautiful young woman whom I love with all my heart, but can do nothing about!

The sad thing about this time in my life that I had to find out only a few years ago, was that the first AA meeting opened in Dartmouth, which is just across the harbour from Halifax, in 1948 and, maybe if someone had questioned my drinking, I might have done something about it, but that is like saying: " If your auntie had balls, she'd be your uncle!" there was no way I'd have accepted help at that time, an alcoholic was someone who drank every day and couldn't stop. I was young and healthy and still in control, or so I thought! The other thing about this was that every time the squadron had a smoker we actually passed the meeting place to get there! I know this because on my bucket list was to revisit Halifax and I did so last August for two weeks. I arrived there on Saturday, 20th and realised that this was my 37th AA birthday; I explained that on Christmas Eve 1956, I had been thrown out of the submarine service and sent back to General service 60 years previously and that I thought enough time had passed for most of the inhabitants to forget. The other thing that really saddened me was that 892 Robie was no longer there, just an empty space where it used to be! I was going to apologise for digressing again but have decided against it as it will keep you up to date as to where I am in real time, I only hope it doesn't stop you from reading on when you find out how much farther this has to go! I promise you, it does get much better, remember I told you I am the eternal optimist!

By this time Sheila and Sylvia have settled into 892, Robie and are well pleased with our choice of accommodation and have settled which rooms are whose, with personal effects they have brought with them. Sheila has got herself a job as a night nursing supervisor in the local children's hospital which helps with the extra costs as we still have to settle the bills ourselves! We are still exercising in the Bermuda area and after a couple of trips, we are into May and springtime is upon us! It happened overnight, we went to bed one night with the place still covered in snow and woke up to green grass and not a bit of snow to be seen, I'd never seen anything like it, even in Scotland with the weather we'd been used to! After the girls arrived, Don decided to get himself a car and purchased a little Austin A30 and I decided to get myself one, I'd seen a Hillman MInx advertised for sale at $100 and got one of the stokers to come with me to check it out. We arrived at the address and there it was looking good, everything seemed to be in fairly good condition and when I got into the driving seat and the stoker into the passenger side, we looked for the handbrake and when we couldn't find it the stoker said: "Maybe this model doesn't have one." I knew nothing about cars and I couldn't even drive at this point, so I took his word for it, after all, he was the expert. Anyway, we agreed to take it at the bargain price and the expert drove it back to 892, Robie and parked it on the drive. I decided to get some driving lessons and there was a lieutenant in the Canadian Navy, living opposite and he volunteered to help. Opposite 892 and about 50 yards up there was a junction, where we could make a right turn, drive to the bottom of a fairly steep hill, turn right, drive about 150 yards and turn right again, up to the top turn right and we would have completed a square. That was the plan and we set off with me in the driving seat and completed the square with the lieutenant white as a sheet and asking how on earth I had managed to navigate a car with practically no brakes and no handbrake round those corners. There were no more driving lessons, at least not in that car and eventually it went for scrap after the lack of brakes couldn't stop it rolling into the back garden, when I took it too far up the drive and left it on a slope! I still have a photograph of about six of us trying to get it out!

I was a bit more cautious about the next car, it was an MG midget, 1953 model and this was 1955. It really was a smart little car and I knew what to look for this time. It cost $1100 and was in excellent condition, I learnt to drive in this car and it was a joy to drive. I still have the workshop manual that I bought so that I could tinker about under the bonnet and the only thing I had to do with it was to replace the starter motor which had given up and after replacing it, I had no more trouble. The only other time I had trouble was when drink was involved! We had been to a smoker over in Dartmouth and I'd got quite drunk, when we arrived home there was a bit of an argument about my drinking and I took off in a huff. I got in the car and took off, I was intending to drive around Bedford Basin and back in order to cool down. I was driving along when suddenly it felt like the front suspension had gone and I had no steering, when I applied the brakes, the car just swung round and reversed into a tree. I think somebody came along and gave me a lift back home because the car had to be left there as it couldn't be driven. I think I have Don to thank for getting me out of the biggest mess I'd been in so far. When I got home and went into the bedroom where Sheila was asleep, I woke her up and said: "I think I've hurt myself," and she just said: "it serves you right!" but when she saw me and examined me, my groin was open and the femoral artery was exposed, I didn't know this at the time as she just went into her nursing role and got me to the sick bay or hospital, I'm not sure which! Surprisingly, there was no repercussion after the event and I was too ashamed of my behaviour to talk about it afterwards, I'm sure it was Don who kept it quiet and I'm just sorry that I never got the opportunity to thank him.

CHAPTER 15

Some of you who are reading this, having stuck it out so far, might have noticed that my life has been a series of disasters, with the result that a lot of my time has been spent trying to understand what went wrong and, not knowing what to do about it, I became resigned to the fact that my life would carry on, going from disaster to disaster. At the time of writing, all that is behind me, as will become apparent in time as the story unfolds. My experience has left me with a philosophy on life that I am quite comfortable with because I have a lifestyle that doesn't make too many demands on my time and I have a freedom that I never thought was possible. Everything in life can be simplified, as long as we remember that to keep it simple, we first have to get it simple and that can be quite complicated as was shown during my initial training in electrical school, when it took two huge blackboards to convert a mess of numbers, letters and symbols to $X = 5$!

The MG was back on the road and things had settled down again and the weather was fine enough so that we could get out and about the countryside surrounding Halifax when we were both off duty. Life was good and I was behaving like a responsible husband, when Sheila took ill and was taken into hospital, they discovered that she had adhesions in her intestines, which meant an operation which meant a few weeks off work. The operation went well and she made a good recovery and the hospital staff were wonderful, the surgeon didn't charge for his services! Considering how short a time she had been with them, it was a measure of her popularity that she was so well thought of. I think during that time, I realised how fragile life was and what would I have done, if I'd lost her, it made me think of how selfish my behaviour had become, considering all the times my life had been on a knife edge because of my drinking, without thinking what it would have done to Sheila and, for the first time I decided to make a promise to myself, that things would be different in the future! I'd made this kind of promise thousands of times in the past to all sorts of people, knowing that I wouldn't be able to keep them but I was hoping it would be different this time! It wasn't that I was in denial, I really was unaware just how powerful this illness has on your thinking. It is the only illness that I know of, that can convince you don't have it because time after time your head is telling you that one drink can't hurt you! I know now that isn't true but I still have years ahead of me, getting trapped every time with this insane thinking. I know this because it is my experience and I wouldn't be true to myself if I didn't pass this knowledge on, so if you recognise the symptoms, please find a number of your nearest AA meeting, it could save your life!

It is so obvious from what I have just written that I was unable to keep that promise to myself that I was so sure I could and, towards the end of this year, our marriage would be in a very precarious position, again because I'd succumbed to the first drink! While reliving this time, I feel more guilty than ever because it is so obvious that I have no one left to blame for the predicament we are in. All our plans for another 12 months in Halifax, Sheila's new job and friends will have come to nothing. I just thank God that Sheila did not decide to just let me go and get on with her own life, which I would never have blamed her for! This happened because I had been caught drunk on watch one night and arguing with the duty officer that I wasn't. The result was that I was remanded for a warrant to be read out on board HM Submarine Alliance, which I was part of the crew then, on Christmas Eve, 1956! The warrant was duly read out by Freddie Fox, Commander SM in the fore ends with the officers and senior rates behind him and me facing them with the junior rates behind me. I can't remember the precise wording of the warrant, but it meant the loss of my leading rate and good conduct badge and out of the submarine service and back to General Service on January 17 1957! So here I am, reduced to the ranks, never thinking that it would come to this but, looking back on my life, it was inevitable that it had to happen, a service like the Royal Navy would only stand for so much and I had to admit, in spite of my early dreams, I had become what is known as a hazard to shipping! The morning after, being Christmas Day, I went aboard to get my gear and to strip my badges off my uniform. While I was there, the rum ration was there and I got a lot of sympathy and quite a few sips of rum! The officers were having cocktails in the wardroom with a few lady friends, I placed my discarded badges on a saucer, took them along to the wardroom, opened the curtain and placed them on the table, wished them all a very merry Christmas, walked into the control room, had a pee down a handy voice pipe and left the boat!

The next time I was to enter the fore ends of that submarine was in February, 1997 when Sheila and I had rented a cottage near Eastbourne for a week and revisited our earlier days there, a lot of wonderful memories and something that was just a spur of the moment thing at the time but very timely as you will be aware as the story unfolds! We visited Brighton and met up with Alma, Sheila's nursing friend who had met and married a native of Brighton and had stayed on. We went from there to Gosport where Alliance was the centre piece of the Royal Navy Museum and we went aboard, very strange feelings when standing on the very spot where those fateful words were read out all those years ago! Both sweet and sour as we were in a different place and time! Anyway, back to where I was and the time has come for my departure, Thursday, 17th January 1957. I remember it well because as I was leaving Stadacona for the last time to get a taxi to the station, the driver told me that my right ear lobe was frozen! I pinched it between my finger and thumb and could hear and feel the ice crackling! I had arranged to get to Montreal by train and from the Canadian Air Force Base there, I was scheduled on a flight to Nottingham, England via Prestwick in Scotland. As my sister was getting married on the 18th, I had arranged to report to Devonport on the Monday and Prestwick being only about twenty miles from Cumnock; it felt like things were going to be alright! The train journey from Halifax to Montreal was fairly uneventful but my thoughts were very much on recent events, wondering how I was going to explain my sudden and unexpected return. When we arrived in Montreal the temperature was -25 degrees C and I passed a church which had recently been on fire, covered in ice, even the arcs of frozen water from the hoses still there and I wished I'd had a camera with me!

Again I had got it wrong when I said it looked as if things were looking up, the night before we were due to take off the flight plan was changed, instead of Prestwick, it was Gander in Newfoundland, getting into Nottingham on Friday the 18th, too late to get back to Cumnock, missing my sister's wedding and having to stay the weekend in Nottingham. On the Saturday, I had to pass the time somehow and I heard that Nottingham Forest were at home so I decided to take in the football match. There was a pub on the corner opposite the ground and I went in for just a half of beer the bar consisted of one bar, in a kind of oval shape, so that when you were having your drink, you were watching the people on the opposite of the oval. Imagine my surprise when I spotted Brian Mulvey, a stoker who had been on the Alderney with me in Halifax just a few months previously. I couldn't believe my eyes and, when we got talking, it turned out that he lived in Nottingham and we went to the game together. Afterwards, he took me and introduced me to his family and I spent a couple of hours with them which was very nice, then I left because I had booked into a B&B for the night.

I don't think that I waited till Monday but decided I'd travel on the Sunday and report to Reserve Fleet where I would stay till they found something for me to do!

I don't think it was too long till I knew that Sheila was on her way home and I had to organise some digs locally till we could get into married quarters. I found a flat in Keyham, which left a lot to be desired but would do as a temporary abode and was within walking distance of the dockyard. Life in reserve fleet was pretty boring and my job for part of the time was to go up the river Tamar to run the generator that produced the electricity to provide the lighting on the ships that were known as the trot, tied up bow to stern in a long line, amongst them the famous old battleship from Exercise Mainbrace, Vanguard. I remember one day going aboard her and what an eerie feeling that was! All her armaments had been stripped and between decks, everything was stripped bare. I was the only person on board and the sound of my footsteps rang out like I was inside a bell! It was a very emotional time, trying to remember what it was like when she was operational and all the proud moments of history she had been privy to!

Anyway, life went on and Sheila arrived at our humble abode in Keyham and it wasn't too long before we were allocated a married quarter at 51 Poole Park Road, St. Budeaux. It was in a block of six and we were allocated the right hand, third floor flat. We were the very first tenants and it was a lovely two bedroom flat with a balcony off the kitchen, overlooking the garden and we had it for three years! Sheila wasn't too long before she got back into her nursing career and found a job in the local children's hospital where she met and befriended a lovely Irish woman, name Kitty Yuill who was married to the manager of one of the local Naval Tailors called, wait for it, Clem! They were a lovely couple and we became very close friends and kept in touch over the years till sadly, they passed away quite a number of years ago, as they were both quite a bit older than us.

One of my favourite pastimes was fishing while I was up the trot, I'd get a line with a hook attached, strip a bit of red cable insulation, slide it up the hook and wait till the tide was on the turn, then float it on the surface and caught loads of lovely sea bass that way, they just couldn't resist it!. You had to be very careful when handling them, their dorsal fins had very sharp and strong spikes that had been known to pierce through the soles of shoes!

CHAPTER 16

I didn't know it at this time, but apart from about time spent in Liverpool on HMS Camperdown, undergoing a refit, I wouldn't leave Devonport again till I left the Navy, almost four years later! I'll spend some of this chapter telling you about the few months in Liverpool and how this illness followed me there. It didn't seem to matter how many geographic changes I made, I couldn't escape me or my illness and I'd become resigned to the fact that it was never going to be different! This was just like a rerun of Invergordon but it lasted a couple of months where Invergordon was only for six weeks, a bit more time and a lot more city! Like Invergordon, there were just about the same number and maybe a few less than the three crews in Invergordon, a total of eighteen and I think there were less than a dozen standing by Camperdown and our duties were laughable, consisting of, showing up every day, going to the same ware house and spending a couple of hours, counting the inventory that was already stored there, to make sure nothing was missing! Afterwards, we'd retire to the local tavern where quite often there would be a lock in when they closed at two thirty and we'd still be there when they reopened at five! The dock road in Liverpool at this time was just as it been for decades, the overhead railway was still there and there were still thousands of dock workers spilling out of the gates at clocking off time. If it hadn't been for the different language, you would have thought you were in Glasgow, the sense of humour of the Liverpudlians was almost identical to the Glaswegians and it was a very happy city. Because we were away from our base, we were paid subsistence allowance, which was added to our fortnightly pay and, depending how much our digs cost, we could have a fair amount of extra money to spend. I was staying with Don's in-laws as I didn't fancy living with my in-laws because I didn't get on too well with my mother-in-law and I didn't want her watching my every move. I had always got on well with Sylvia's parents and they refused to take any dig money and I didn't make too much of a fight. I was still a selfish B and always thinking of myself, although my conscience was tormenting me constantly and the only way I could quiet it was to use my short term solution and forget everything in drink!

We are now into 1958 and I had to leave Sheila again to be in Liverpool from sometime in January, I'm not very good at remembering dates, but I knew we had been there for a few weeks before we heard of the Munich disaster when a crowd of Busby Babes were killed. We were expecting to be in Liverpool for quite some time, but I was recalled to Devonport and it wasn't till I got there that I found out that I had been selected to be part of the combined service team to be observers on Christmas Island during the nuclear bomb testing for which we had to sign the official secrets act. Knowing what I know now about those tests, I am grateful that I suffered a broken collar bone and was unable to take part! But at least it got me back to Devonport and Sheila, she always seemed to have a steadying effect on my drinking. This was the year that my drinking really had an adverse effect on my health and I was starting to suffer from severe stomach pains, which made me cut down to not drinking for weeks at a time. All during this time, we had been trying for a family but it turned out that Sheila was unable to conceive and we had started talking about adoption and decided to go ahead and apply. This meant a lot of background investigation and I immediately thought that with my history, we'd be turned down. However, they requested a report from my divisional officer, who asked if it would be alright if he paid us a visit, telling us what it was about. Of course, we agreed and the day came when he showed up and I was on my best behaviour. We had a pet budgie called tinker who was rarely in his nest and took great delight in landing on our visitor's head and lifting a strand of his hair, much to our dismay but he took it all in good part and ended up giving us a glowing report and we were approved as prospective parents and just had to wait for a suitable child to become available! Obviously, we were both delighted, especially Sheila There was just one blot on the horizon, I had been drafted to HMS Delight, a Daring class destroyer, which after running up exercises, was destined for a two and a half year commission in the Med. I had a great job there, working with the chief EA who was in charge of the fire control computer system and my job was to look after the telemetry systems. This was one of the first computer systems in the service, transistors and op amps hadn't been invented, not even printed circuit boards, it was all done with valve amplifiers in three rows about eight feet high in a room the size of the lounge I'm sitting in at the moment. By this time I had my leading rate back as well as my good conduct badge, which reminds me of an incident earlier when I had been part of reserve fleet. C-inC Plymouth was coming aboard for an inspection, during which time, his flag lieutenant would pick on a few unfortunates to lay their kit out for inspection. Our branch regulating chief who was a chief electrician had been on at me for weeks to let him see that I had all my kit and I kept telling him that I had it all and that it would be there on the day. Imagine my horror when the flag lieutenant tapped me on the shoulder and told me in a quiet voice: "please lay out your kit," and moved on! It was nothing to my relief when he returned a few seconds later and apologised, he hadn't noticed the leading rate on my right arm. Obviously, he had failed to notice that there was nothing on my left arm! That was really a lucky escape because I'd been bluffing the chief all along, I had just enough kit to get me through my week!

Anyway, back to the task at hand, we were busy doing gunnery trials and I'd still been having those troubling stomach pains, I saw the ship's doctor and he wanted me to report to Stone house (the Naval hospital in Devonport) the next morning at nine o'clock where he had arranged a barium meal and X-ray. I asked my divisional officer if I could go home and attend the hospital from there, he told me that he'd rather I stayed because the trials were continuing till later in case anything went wrong. I think that was the first time I was told that I was really needed and I was chuffed to bits! I was taken ashore the next morning and delivered to Stone house at the appointed hour, examined by a doctor and prepared for X-ray after drinking about a pint of barium liquid, which tasted horrible. After the X-ray, I was told that I had a duodenal ulcer the size of a golf ball and I was taken to a ward by wheel chair and put to bed for three weeks bed rest on a milk only diet! If my head wouldn't do anything about the abuse I was giving my body, then certainly my body would take charge, by saying: "enough is enough, this has to stop!" I was in hospital for three months, discharged but stopped draft for three months to see how it progressed.

It was during this period that we received a letter from the adoption people, saying that they had found a suitable child and would we like to attend the foster home where he was being cared for? The foster home was in Exmouth and we went there at the earliest opportunity, the foster home was like a run-down country house and the foster mother was a lovely, elderly lady who introduced us to a little 5 week old boy and after being told that he was prone to a slight tendency of travel sickness, he was a very healthy little boy and, if we were agreeable, we could take him home with us that day! We were both absolutely delighted and I'll never forget sitting opposite Sheila, just watching her holding our baby boy and feeling how much love she felt for that baby at that moment. That picture has never left me to this day! We had already decided on his name, he was to be called Alexander after Sheila's dad and James after my dad, so Alexander James McMillan became, in a relatively short time, known as Wee Eck and subsequently as Big Eck! But we never called him that, it was always Alex.

In the meantime, my health was improving, as long I watched what I was eating, it just took something like a hamburger and it flared up again, it felt like my digestive system was shot to hell and I was slowly coming to terms with the fact that the only solution would be surgery and, after another couple of spells in the medical ward, I was given the option of either a medical discharge or an operation. I chose the operation because, if I went out with a medical condition, I would probably spend more time off work and I didn't want that, and after the operation, I would be fit enough to stay in the navy. So I was transferred to the surgical ward along with a little Scottish seaman PO, for the same operation. When we got there, to our surprise, there was a dockyard matey who had followed us through most of our medical visits without finding anything wrong, I got the impression that he was a hypochondriac and he told us that he was there for an operation on his knee. I told him that he should ask the surgeon to examine his intestines while he was under the anaesthetic. There was a hook over the operating table that they used to pass the intestines over so that they could examine every inch and if something was not right, they would find it! I don't know whether he believed me or not but I could see he was thinking about it.

The operation I was scheduled for was called a partial gastrectomy, which meant removal of half my stomach and my duodenum, which was discontinued a few years later for a less drastic solution. About this time, the tenancy of our married quarter would shortly terminate and we'd have to find alternative accommodation. After a short time, while I was still in hospital, Sheila told me that she'd put a deposit down on a semi-detached two bedroom bungalow off Child-wall Five ways in Liverpool and all I had to do was sign the mortgage agreement! I was very happy to do this because, for the first time in our married life, we'd have a real home with a real family!

The day of the operation arrived, I was prepped and taken from the ward to the operating theatre, where I was given a pre-op injection that made me feel a bit light headed and I didn't care what they were going to do to me! Then came the real anaesthetic and I remember nothing, till I woke up in the ward some hours later with the nurse asking me if I was alright and that it had all gone well, I don't know how long afterwards that I asked her if I would be able to play the accordion after such an operation and she told me: "Certainly" to which I replied: "Good, I couldn't play one when I came In!" I think it was my sense of humour that got me through a lot of the difficult periods of my life, possibly without it, I would probably have given up.

CHAPTER 17

We are now into late 1959 and I've been drafted from reserve fleet back into HMS Drake, where I am put in charge of the ELP or electric light party, which was a bit of a joke as there about three pensioners employed to do the same thing! We just let them get on with it and spent our time playing cards! I had that job for quite a few months until they made me the caterer of the transit mess, which is full of junior rates, waiting for draft or, like me, stopped draft for health or other reasons. My only duties are very simple, like making sure there is no trouble in the mess and lights out are on time and everyone is up and about their duties on time. The only other duty I have to do is clip everyone's rum card when they get their tot, to make sure they don't get more than one! Tot time is quite a ritual for junior rates, there is the rum bosun, who measures out 1 measure of rum to 2 measures of water into one glass and the PO who sees to it that they drink it! there was one day when I was doing my duty when I was asked if I'd had mine, I said no and he said: "you'd better get yours now when it's quiet," he then put 2 measures of rum and 1 measure of water into my glass and I drank it! This was repeated a few times till I answered in the affirmative. As far as I can remember, this only happened the one time, I wish it hadn't because it had consequences that I'd rather forget! Because I was mess caterer, this carried a perk that allowed me a make and mend or an afternoon off, so after lunch, I proceeded towards The St Leven's pub for a couple of pints. After a couple, I decided to make my way to the Prince of Wales, where my old Chief of the kit muster saga, was now landlord! I had crossed over to the side opposite Albert gate and within sight of my destination when I was overcome with that familiar feeling that your stomach needs to evacuate most of the excesses it has had to suffer! Unfortunately, there is an elderly couple in front of me and he looks like a navy pensioner as he is wearing his old navy raincoat, plus the fact, he is on crutches because he has only one leg. They are right in front of the door into the Prince of Wales when my stomach decided it couldn't wait and I threw up all down the back of his raincoat. By the time he turned around I was into the Prince of Wales and straight through to the toilet. I couldn't imagine what he thought when he turned around and there was nobody there!

From this, you'll have guessed that I have recovered enough to start drinking again and my life has reverted to the same old, same old! I have now survived into 1960, much to my surprise and I'm now into my 10th year of service and my life is a mess, the only good thing about life is that Sheila is still in it and our son Alex. What a difference to the young 18 year old and his dreams of glory! Here I am, ducking and diving, making excuses to people I owe money to and making up stories to tell to strangers, that they might feel sorry for me and lend me money that I know they haven't a chance of ever seeing again. Whenever I think of all the people who were victims of my deceit, what I said in the prologue, if any marks I left were on you, I am sincerely sorry! If, by any chance, any victims of my deceit read this, please get in touch and allow me to make amends.

It was about this time that I discovered my mother was dying of cancer and I was given compassionate leave to be with her. When I found out that she had been misdiagnosed two years previously, I wanted to go and find the doctor and kill him, fortunately, I was stopped because I had such a rage in me that I knew I was capable of murder! I was with her when she died and her last words to me were: "Iain, will you try and stay out of the pubs and look after your dad?" She was only 49 years old and just ready to start enjoying life, after raising 7 children when she was so cruelly taken. Is it any wonder that I was angry?

When I got back from my compassionate leave, I was declared fit for draft, so here I am, wondering what was to come next, when a draft chit came through, sending me to HMS Tiger a brand new super tech cruiser, which I definitely had no wish to join, so I reported sick again and was given the chance of a medical discharge, which I jumped at. It was the best geographical escape I could think of and it couldn't have come at a better time. After all the necessary papers were signed, my leaving date, allowing for sick leave and termination leave was set for the 25th of November, the day after my 28th birthday. I remember getting the train for the last time from Plymouth North Road to Reading, where the final demobilisation would take place. I was kitted out with a full set of civilian clothes, comprising of a three piece suit, 2 shirts, collarless, 4 collars 2 sets of collar studs, back and front, underwear socks and shoes and a cap or hat of choice and given a rail warrant from Reading to Liverpool, and my Navy career had come to an end! Not quite, because I was still in the navy till my two months leave was up and that would take me to about the end of February, almost exactly 10 years' service! When I arrived in Liverpool and showed up at 2 Wallgate Way as a civilian wearing my brand new demob suit, it must have been quite funny for Sheila, seeing me as a civilian for the very first time in her life! I certainly felt different and the first thing I had to consider was finding work of some sort. I still had two months of Navy pay, so there was no immediate rush. I wanted to get started as soon as possible though and I got a job as a maintenance electrician at Pilkington Glass Works in St. Helens. It was a very dirty job and long hours because I had to get two buses to get there and back. I stuck it out for a month and decided to get something nearer home. I was very lucky because the electrical contractor who had the contract for the installation of services on the site of our house was looking for electricians, I applied and was given the job. I absolutely hated the job, I just couldn't get to grips with the skills required for that kind of job, but I stuck it out for about six months and told the gaffer that I was never going to be a benefit to his business and he would be better off if he let me go and he seemed quite happy to agree!

One thing I remember about this time, which I find strange, is that I wasn't drinking. I don't recall ever going into a pub there, I didn't mix with my workmates who would likely go for a pint after work so the temptation to drink wasn't there! I don't think, although I can't be sure, that I gave it too much thought, I was just happy to be at home with my family, although the job prospects was a bit of a worry.

I talked things over with Sheila and we both agreed that I should enquire about job prospects in the Merchant Navy as I still had that desire for a life at sea! Being in Liverpool at that time meant that there were still lots of British companies registered there and I found out that Canadian Pacific were looking for junior electrical officers, I applied and found that I was 9th electrical officer on MV Empress of Canada for her 3rd transatlantic voyage between Liverpool and Montreal, calling in at Glasgow to pick up more passengers who were taking advantage of the £10 immigration passage that was being offered at that time. What a shock to the system that was, I was an officer with a thin gold stripe on my sleeves and that was nothing to the feelings when I saw the ship that I was to be part of the crew of, for the first time. The opulence was something else, like a 5-star hotel and our saloon was next to the first class saloon with the same menu. All this for someone who has come from the submarine service and survived for a week on mashed potatoes and tinned beetroot!

This proved to be a bad move as we were allowed to order alcohol and beer from the bond and the cost was deducted from our wages. As usual, I went overboard and ordered too much, like a bottle of whisky and a case of beer, so I shouldn't have been surprised when I was taken to task about my drinking! It was obvious that I wasn't going to last too long on a passenger ship, I was lucky to last three trips before I was transferred to the Beaver Cove, one of their fleet of cargo ships, they sailed out of London to Montreal across the North Atlantic and our job was to service as many of the deck winches as we could on the passage out, there was a chief electrician and myself to do this work, it was alright in good weather but hellish in the cold and rain! The electric controls were in a sealed box, with a heavy steel lid, secured by about two dozen bolts which was the longest part of the job, getting them out, lifting the lid, checking all the contacts inside, repairing any faults found and making sure the lid was sealed and watertight before replacing the bolts, making sure they were well greased, so that they didn't get rusted in. I hated the job but it had to be done and I was glad when it was over. The other thing I didn't like about the beaver boats was that they were very dirty animals and, whenever they blew the boiler tubes, the boiler room filled with soot, getting everywhere! It was on the Beaver Cove that the thought of suicide first became an option. I remember it vividly, as I do so many other times. I had to go ashore to sign articles and got drinking with the bosun and carried on when we got back on board, that was where the engineering superintendent found me to tell me I was sacked when we got back home! I remember arguing with him and the next thing I remember was waking up and hearing the throb of the engines, I panicked because I knew I should have been down there for leaving harbour! My cabin was on the boat deck and I went out on deck to face a dark, cold, November night, somewhere on the Thames Estuary, watching the green lights of phosphorescence in the ship's wake and praying for the courage to jump overboard! I think the only reason I didn't was because of the temperature of the water!

I am not going to spend a lot of time getting through the next six or seven years as there is just a lot of the same, I covered a lot of ground, not seeing much of it. What I will do is to list the companies I sailed with, not too many for a second trip!

I was sacked by Canadian Pacific when we returned to the UK and, instead of looking for another ship, I decided to try and get work in Liverpool, but there didn't seem to be too much about, so we decided to up sticks again, sell up and move back to Cumnock. We had paid £2,400 for the bungalow and sold it for £3,200 so we had a bit of cash in hand. When we arrived back in Cumnock, we lived with my mum and dad in their new house, 212, Barrhill Road, which was a beautiful semi-detached dormer bungalow, being one of only six like it. We weren't there long before I found that my service had kept me at the top of the council housing list and we were housed within a few weeks in a brand new bungalow in a new development, just being built and we didn't have to buy for some time as the rent was fair, we had both been brought up in council houses, so we were quite happy and we had good neighbours!

CHAPTER 18

So, here we are back, looking for another ship, but this time in another pool, namely the Broomielaw in Glasgow, where I found one with an old established shipping company called Lyle Shipping Company. The ship I was to join was the MV Cape Horn, discharging cargo at Runcorn Dock on the Liverpool ship canal, just outside Manchester. She was destined to sail in Ballast to Tampa, Florida and then on to Newcastle, NSW in Australia. The trip was supposed to last approximately 9 months but it was just over 13 months before we got home! This was the ship, described in chapter 12, so enough said about her, except to give you some idea of what the crew was like, we arrived Tampa and stayed overnight to take on a cargo of grain for Newcastle, I didn't go ashore and when I got up in the morning to find the bosun locked up in the tally clerk's office for beating up one of the deck cadets, he was kept there for the remainder of the voyage, his meals served by the skipper and when we arrived in Newcastle he was collected by the police and we heard no more about him. Just to give another example, 19 of the crew jumped ship and we were left with the remainder being DBS's (distressed British Seamen) Obviously I wasn't invited back for a second trip and my next ship was with Houlder Brothers, after a fair bit of leave time when I joined one of the company's ore carriers, going out to Almeria in Spain to pick up iron ore and back to the UK. I didn't do another trip with that company, I decided I liked the tramping companies better. The next company I joined was not a tramping company but a general cargo ship and the company was Trinder Anderson and the ship was MV Limerick. When I joined her she was already loaded with cargo bound for most of the major ports in Australia, including a huge amount of military equipment for Townsville in Northern Queensland where a big military exercise was planned. Starting on the west coast, it took weeks to get to Townsville, a few days to unload and then about the same time in reverse, collecting cargo bound for the UK. Although I didn't know it at the time, this was to be my swan song, and I wouldn't find out until a few months after I was home. We are now into January 1967 and I am having an extended leave, to make up for the time I've been away. I don't remember how long after when I had a phone call from one of the engineers who had been on the Cape Horn with me, he said they were going to join a ship and did I want to join them? I asked them about it and was told it was a good job, so I said OK, I'll make enquiries. It was when I went up to the Broomielaw to sign on, that I found that I was blacklisted, not only in that pool but in every pool in the UK! I think I made my feelings clear in chapter 12, so from here we'll be in a different place!

We are now into the spring of 1970 and I am still working with George Rutherford when he tells me that he's been thinking of joining the Merchant Navy and could I help him? I said I'd take him up to what is now Scottish Ship Management, an amalgamation of Lyles, Hogarth's and another English company that ran the Temple ships. Their offices are in Prince's Square just off Buchanan Street and I said I'd take him there as he doesn't drive. I managed to get parked in Prince's Square and took George up to the office, where he had arranged an appointment, somebody collected him and, while I was waiting for him, Captain Love, the deck superintendent came into reception and recognised me. He asked me what I was doing and did I not want to get back to sea? When I told him I'd love to, he said that they were looking for electricians and the job was mine if I wanted it. I told him of my previous behaviour and that I'd stopped drinking and was a member of AA for over six months. I got the job, gave in my notice and joined the Baron Cawder with George as 2nd electrician! I wasn't expecting that because it meant that I was now his boss and he didn't like it, especially since I'd stopped drinking and wasn't so easy to manipulate! There was one time when we were ashore in Amsterdam and I was trying to keep an eye on him when he turned on me and called me for everything. I had the feeling that his anger was because I wasn't the person he had got used to and didn't like it. However, I let it go and decided that was the last time I'd go ashore with him, he could get on with it and I'd just have to live with it till the end of the trip and he'd get his own ship! There was the danger that I would become "Holier than Thou" so I had to tread carefully because he was an old friend and I didn't want to damage that.

I was thinking of all this last night when it suddenly occurred to me that I had missed out a very significant period in the sixties. This was the time when I had a season ticket to the Ailsa Hospital in Ayr, the local asylum. It was never for my drink problem, it was for nervous debility or some other stress related illness. My memory of this time is very sketchy as I was given electric shock therapy from time to time. I actually came to love it, because it totally wiped my memory and it gave me a sort of peace I'd always dreamed of, but it only lasted for about half an hour and then the memories came flooding back in! There is a saying that tells us that the road to Hell is paved with good intentions, but my experience is telling me that the opposite is true and it is the road to Heaven that is paved with good intentions. All my life, my intentions were of the best and they got me to be where I have to be, in a place and time I was destined to be! This incident that I am about to relate was also very well intentioned, I decided that I would try another geographic by going to Coventry where there was plenty of work and make a new start. I set off, looking every bit the successful individual that people would be mad if they didn't employ!

I found a very respectable bed and breakfast and booked myself in, found a job within a couple of days in a ministry of defence place, working with ex Royal Navy electrical equipment that I was already familiar with. The drinking started again and I soon found myself out of the B&B as they were too respectable for the likes of me and I ended up in a working man's hostel, where I shared a room with a middle aged man who was very quiet and went out to work every day and didn't drink, which was unusual as everybody else there seemed to. My drinking progressed to the point where I'd work for a couple of days, collect my money and when that was spent, find another job for a couple of days and continue on the merry-go-round until a letter arrived from Sheila and when I opened it there was just a single sheet of paper and scrawled in a childish hand a note from Alex who had just started school, saying: "Please come home, daddy, we both miss you very much, love Alex." I think I had sent home one payment of only five ponds and when I read that note from my son I felt such a sense of self-loathing that I screwed the note up and threw it in the bin. But the note had served its purpose; I packed everything up and headed home to beg their forgiveness again. it was while I was living in the hostel that, one night I couldn't sleep, tormented by guilt and shame, the sheets all twisted round me and I don't know whether I shouted out loud or just in my thoughts, but it came from my heart and I said: "please God, Help me!" I think it was only a day or so after when the letter arrived. I haven't much recollection of what happened when I got home but as this is just a remembering, things must have sorted themselves out and we are where we are again. I am now on contract with the company, so we decided it is now time to buy again and we find a place in Troon which is on the coast and just a couple of miles from Ayr.

My next ship was the Cape Hawke, she had just completed a refit after she had been storm damaged, she had what was known as a pooped wave hit her stern on and flooded all the accommodation, so she was like brand new and had been fitted with twin medium speed diesels and variable pitch propellers. This was what was known a pier head jump as she had to leave without an electrician and I had to join her at sea, which meant I had to fly out to Las Palmas, stay the night in a hotel and get the pilot boat out to meet her as she went slowly ahead and we drew up alongside, it reminded me of when I joined HMS Eagle all those years ago. They threw a jumping ladder over the side followed by a heaving line to haul my baggage on board followed by me on the jumping ladder and we were off to Japan with a cargo of steel tubes. We only got as far as the South Atlantic when the crankshaft on the port engine went and we had to put into Durban, to wait for a re-placement to be sent out and we were actually there for a month. Durban at this time was a lovely city, with loads of great restaurants, the 2nd mate had relatives there and we were invited to a barbeque there one day, they had a fantastic house halfway up the mountainside, overlooking the city and out to sea.

Another time, we were offered a day's sea fishing by a Scot who had emigrated there years ago and owned a ship cleaning business. This was a squad of natives who would descend on the ship after repairs and scrub the engine room clean. Quite an entrepreneur! He had arranged to pick a few of us up at 5am but he phoned to let us know that he had broken down and would get us later. It was actually 8am when he finally got there and took us round to pick up his boat. What a boat, it was a 30 footer with twin 75HP outboards, once aboard he got in touch with friends who were already out to find out where the fish were and we were off, this thing just went bows up, stern down and took off at a rate of knots, we were round the Bluff in a matter of minutes to join the others. All the gear was ready and, after baiting the hooks, the real fun began. There was a boat off to starboard, about 20 feet away, while we were watching someone had a fish on and was reeling it in, it got to a few feet of the stern, when this huge shark took what was probably about a 50 pound fish and the poor fisherman was left with a head to reel in! Shortly after I got a 15lb. barracuda which I managed to land, exciting stuff and we thanked the guy for a great day out when he dropped us off at the ship.

On the 3rd weekend there, the 2nd mate and I rented a car for the weekend, he'd have it on the Saturday and I'd have it on Sunday. On the Sunday, I got one of the deck cadets and we headed up what was known as the valley of a thousand hills. What a trip that was, really wild country and every now and again we'd come across a Zulu village. When I think back to my drinking days, I'm so grateful to have had these four years at sea, sober and to be able to say, it wasn't all wasted!

CHAPTER 19

During my time with SMM, I earned study leave and attended South Shields Marine College on different occasions to obtain a final certificate in Control Engineering and industrial electronics, and as mentioned earlier, gaining a distinction in mathematics! I served on another four ships before deciding to come ashore for good in 1974. I was on a baron boat, running up river in Venezuela to pick up a cargo of bauxite and stockpile it on Trinidad when we had stockpiled enough for a full cargo, we'd reload it and took it to Chicoutimi in Northern Quebec and back to Venezuela. My next job was again in South America, sailing from Chimbote in Peru with cargos of fishmeal to various ports around South and Central America, then there was the time when we were trading around the Gulf ports, carrying various bulk cargos, spent about ten days in Mobile, Alabama where I met with an AA contact, was made very welcome and taken to lots of meetings, making lots of new friends. I also managed a trip up the Mississippi to Baton Rouge for a cargo of some sort of nuts bound for the UK and end of the trip!

My last ship was the MV Cape Leeuwin, the first bridge controlled ship in the fleet, which meant that I would have to fly to Horton in Norway three weeks early for training on the control system, before the Company accepts delivery from the builders, the training went well and by the time of sailing, I had a fair grasp of how the system worked. We sailed from Horton to Rotterdam, where we picked up a cargo of steel tubes for the Arabian Gulf and then on to Christmas Island in the Indian Ocean, where we loaded phosphates for Eastern Australia. Because of Board of Trade rules, we weren't supposed to go unmanned in the engine room until six months of proving the system worked. I can't remember when we found a snag in the system, but it could only have been a few days when, during testing, we found that the fuel lever wasn't responding to commands. The whole of the system software was contained in a steel cube about 24 inches square with a multi meter and control switch to test all the systems. I think I spent at least a couple of days, checking the system and decided that some of the information in the manual was wrong. To tell if the system was working or not, either a full swing of the needle or not, would let you know, one way or another. I then decided to do what I would have done without a manual and that would be to check everything manually. Excuse me if I get a bit technical here, but there is no other way to describe the procedure. The fuel lever was moved by a transducer operated hydraulic ramp. I checked the output current to the transducer and found it to be delivering the correct range of current (8-15ma). A tap with a hammer to the hydraulic ramp cured the problem!

The result of this exercise was that I knew the system inside out and, after making the necessary changes to the manual, I had a word with the chief engineer and we decided that it was safe enough to go unmanned. The system allowed the engineers to leave the system in charge from 5pm till 8am while the engineers took turns to be night aboard as they did when in port. They each had an alarm panel in their respective cabins as did I, which let them know what degree of urgency was required. It was a brilliant system and gave us very little trouble during the rest of the trip. After the steel tubes were delivered, we then sailed for Christmas Island and I was back where I started with Lyle's Shipping, the difference being that we were only articled for a four months voyage instead of the 13 I had done on Cape Horn but with the same itinerary, from Christmas Island, Nauru or Ocean Island in the Pacific to almost every port in Australia. Forgive me, if I've mentioned this elsewhere, but when I was on the Cape

Horn, picking up from Ocean Island, we were caught in the heavy swell season which meant that because it was gantry loading, we couldn't go alongside and had to shut the job down and drift for a couple of days, start the job up and close with the island again. This went on for 49 days, 7 weeks! We caught 56 sharks with meat hooks from the galley and lumps of liver. I got all my deck controls serviced and ended up brown as a berry. The reason we had to wait so long was the number of ships in the queue ahead of us. When the time came for my relief to arrive, I was a bit sorry to leave, she was a lovely ship with great accommodation. I had a day room, bedroom and bathroom all to myself and just aft of the accommodation was the swimming pool! This was a historic moment in my life, for the first time in my life, after all these years at sea, I left a ship with glowing references, and it prompted me to tell my son Alex what to put on my headstone: "God love him, he tried his best!" I have watched various celebrities over time, destroying themselves through this illness, allowing it to kill them and the one thing they had in common was a fantastic talent in their own particular field. Oliver Reed, George Best, Hurricane Higgins and poor old Gazza, who is still battling on! I don't know what it is that kept them fighting, maybe success or fame, I don't know but I thank God for their example; it reminds me that this is still a killer illness and even after all these years, I am still at risk If I don't keep practising these principles in ALL my affairs! This programme tells us that we claim spiritual progress rather than spiritual progress and if Spiritual Perfection is a finite point in space, then a day at a time I am getting closer to perfection and that is what keeps me going and, just maybe that was what God and Lord Kitchener was telling me all those years ago!

I have been busy over the past few weeks, exploring job prospects and have had a couple of offers, one from Babcock's Power in London as a commissioning engineer and one from a company based in Troon, called Dynadrive as an electronics engineer. This is a new company developing control systems for variable speed drives, I decided on the one in Troon because I thought the Babcock's one would require long spells away from home and I'd had enough of that to last a lifetime! After I joined Dynadrive, I discovered that a fair bit of service work was involved but usually not longer than a couple of days. There was one time I had to go to Paris and was there for nearly a week, sorting their problem, successfully, I'm glad to say. I was doing ok until I had to go to a job in London, where a prototype machine was giving a lot of trouble. I got there and booked into a hotel on the Southend road not too far away from the job. The technicalities of this job are too involved to explain here so I'll summarise by stating that everything I tried failed. I got to the job at 9am Monday, worked through till 6pm, back to the hotel for dinner then spent the rest of the evening and into the small hours poring over the drawings for the remainder for the remainder of the week, to no avail, even spending hours on the phone with the designer of the system, following his suggestions and still with no success. Of course, the inevitable happened and I had to be taken off the job because my brain just sort of refused to work anymore and I suffered a period of what is known as Manic Depression or maybe it was just a nervous breakdown!

I spent a couple of weeks in hospital before going back to work where I decided that I had bitten off more than I could chew and handed in my notice. I got a job not long after at Wallacetown Controls in Ayr a test supervisor. Because of my training as a mining electrician, I was familiar with their products and was quite confident to be back in my comfort zone. Before I left Dynadrive, I was sitting in our back garden, admiring my work and thinking: "Look what I have achieved, a new car in the drive, a 14 ft cabin cruiser parked behind the house and a beautiful sunny afternoon in July!" Then came a very dangerous thought that posed no threat at the time, remember what I was talking about just a couple of paragraphs ago, well that was now and this is then and the thought that was in my mind was: "a shandy would be nice," and to this day, I've no idea where that shandy came from but I drank a can of shandy and three weeks later I'm back in the Ailsa Hospital, getting plugged into the mains electric and back to my two favourite phrases: "I'm sorry" and: " I don't know". I was just two months short of my 5th AA birthday when this happened and I haven't fully forgiven myself for what I did to Sheila and Alex! It took me another 5 years to get back to AA, although I kept trying to get back the magic had gone, I didn't belong drinking and I didn't belong in AA. I knew what I'd done wrong, I'd kept a secret from Joe when I was supposed to share all my defects of character, and I had proof of what AA keeps telling us: "Secrets will keep you sick!"

Whenever a newcomer says: "I'm not that bad!" the stock answer is: "Not yet!" My experience has taught me that before you get to the yet, you have to experience the agains, which are much more painful the second time around! It was during this period that I had a second time round when Sheila and Alex were down in Liverpool visiting her dad, as her mum had died in 1972 and he was on his own and so was I! I was alone in the house with the door locked, curtains drawn, two bottles of whisky and a case of beer. As soon as I opened the seal on the first bottle of whisky, I felt the panic rising when I thought where is the next lot coming from! I got in the car and drove to the nearest pub and ordered a bottle of whisky, paid for it and left. I don't know whether it was the pub landlord who was suspicious and phone the police or I had just been unlucky and a motor cycle cop just happened to be in the vicinity and stopped me but I was arrested again for drunk driving, spent the night in jail and was banned for three years! Not too long after that, I was again at that point of desperation where I felt that I was no use to anybody and that the world would be better off without me! What I have omitted to mention was that, as soon as Alex started school, Sheila gave up nursing and trained to become a primary school teacher and was teaching at Moorhead primary school in Troon. Alex was in Secondary at Marr College, so they both left for school for 9 o'clock and got home just after four. I had the full day to carry out my plan. I had enough pills and drink to do the needful and, as soon as they left, I started to self-destruct! The next thing I knew I was waking up in hospital 3 days later, thinking: "Shit, I'm still here!" What I hadn't realised or known about was that Alex had been doing his prelims that day and was let home at lunchtime and came home to find his dad unconscious, he immediately called his mum, who came home and got the ambulance and the rest, as they say, is history!

Before I leave this chapter and move into 1977, another chapter in my life was closing, my brother, Jim, was diagnosed with cancer of the common bile duct and the prognosis wasn't good. But his first daughter, Margaret, was getting married in November and he was determined that he was going to be there to lead her down the aisle and give her away. It was a lovely family wedding, with most of the family getting down to the prison officers estate which reminded me of the married quarters that Sheila and I had occupied in St. Budeaux. Another coincidence occurred her that Jim had related to me earlier when he had been up on holiday when we had all congregated on the beach at Turnery for a family outing. He told me about a new officer that had joined his team and when he asked what he had done before he said he'd worked on cross channel ferries and before that he'd been in the navy, Jim said: "My brother was in the navy" he said: "I was in submarines" Jim said: "so was my brother" he said: " I was in Canada" Jim said: "so was my brother" he said: "what's his name" Jim said: "Iain McMillan" he said: "I'll show you a photograph and you point him out." As I'm writing this I'm looking at the very photograph they were talking about and I recognise Tex who was sent home like me but because he hadn't a leading rate, he did time in detention for his crime which was like mine, drink related. When the wedding took place, Tex attended the reception and, as soon as he entered the room, I recognised him, even though almost twenty years had passed, He was a great pal of Kiwi, Clem's pal and I believe both he and Tex were sent home at the same time.

Sorry about that he said and Jim said but I couldn't resist it because it was just how I heard it!

CHAPTER 20

We are now into 1977 and I'm still at Wallacetown Control Systems but I've been having trouble and after a lot of testing, it was decided that it was gallstones and I needed surgery. It was decided that the operation would be done at Ballochmyle Hospital, where Sheila had been a theatre sister, working with the consultant surgeon, Mr. Cleland who would be doing the necessary through the same scar from my partial gastrectomy and it wouldn't show. It meant that I would be off work for some time and I had some bad news about Jim, it was just a matter of time so I asked the doctor if it would be OK if I went down and stayed with them and he gave me permission as long as I kept in touch with the medical staff who were looking after Jim. I don't think he could have stopped me, even if he'd wanted to! He was determined that he wasn't going to give in and he made me promise to get him his fishing permit for the next season and I did. It was so sad to see him sitting in his bed, practising his casting! By this time most of the family were here and the neighbours must have wondered what was going on every evening with the sounds of laughter coming from Jim's bedroom. We were all sitting around on his bed and we were reliving the past, the younger ones puzzled at what us older ones were laughing about! We had to resort to some stories when it came to getting his signature for certain documents so that his pension wouldn't go to probate as he still was convinced that he was going to be OK. I remember the day when he actually came to terms with his condition, when he asked me if it was the big C and I had to tell him it was and he burst into tears! I felt so sorry for him and all I could do for him was hold him till the grief passed. I think, but can't be sure, that it was then that he gave in and let go of life and passed away peacefully with his wife, Jessie, by his side. I had been downstairs when she came down to let me know and all I felt was a sense of relief, because it had become too painful to watch him suffer and it reminded me again how I felt when our mother had died, almost 17 years previously. His funeral was testament to his life and popularity, with the street lined with prison officers all the way from his house to the main road. I remember Sheila saying that she could hear the sound of bagpipes during the journey, although I was in the same car and didn't hear anything, but strange things happen in life and I just accepted the fact that somehow she had heard bagpipes at an appropriate moment!

It was some time after the funeral when I reflected on my life and decided that I hadn't been much of a big brother to my younger siblings, when in fact I hadn't been much of anything to society in general!

This was the year when Elvis died and I remember the day at work when the news broke, there were women crying all over the place and I just couldn't understand what all the fuss was about and wondered why the bosses just didn't send them home, because there didn't seem to be any work getting done for the remainder of the day! I was still in my associate membership period at this time, having one of my dry periods and still without my driving licence. This didn't pose too much of a problem at the time as we were still living in Troon and the bus service to Ayr was quite good, but this was to end when I applied for and got a job with the Greater Glasgow Health Board as a hospital engineer at Knightswood Hospital in the spring of 1978. This would mean another move to the North side of Glasgow, but it would have to wait till I got my licence back in order to go house hunting and I spent the next couple of months travelling by train and bus, which wasn't as bad I thought it would be. I remember the day I went for the interview which was conducted by the District Engineer, Alan Grey who had been a chief engineer at sea as had most engineers working for the G.G.H.B at this time, having come through the rigours of an apprenticeship in the Glasgow shipyards and subsequent watch keeping duties with various shipping companies, which proved to be the ideal background required for this type of work. Even though my expertise was of the electrical variety, I had worked alongside enough engineers, both inside and outside the crankcase of huge marine diesel engines, that I could turn my hand to almost any job in the engine room. In fact, during my time on Cape Leeuwin, I had considered, quite seriously, doing enough watch keeping time to earn study leave and go for an engineering certificate, but the desire to be at home with Sheila and Alex won out and so, here I am, still working with marine engineers without getting my feet wet!

One of the questions he asked was: "If you had to sack a member of a trade union, how would you go about it?" I was surprised by the question and should have guessed there was a hint here about the nature of the job ahead of me but, after thinking for a moment I replied: "Very carefully!" which seemed to satisfy him. After reporting for my first day on the job, I was told that the senior engineer was on long term sick leave. There was another engineer already there but I suspected, by the way he spoke, I would soon be on my own! It turned out I was right because shortly afterwards, he left and I got the impression that somehow drink was involved in either his or the sector engineer's decision! I had yet to meet the sector engineer, Malcolm Breen, who was an extremely capable engineer and quite a hard taskmaster who, when I first met him, told me to watch my back, which kind of put my back up and didn't bode well for our future relationship. I got the impression that he was at war at war with trade unions and maybe that was where the question in my interview had come from! All I wanted to do was to go to my work, find out what the day's priorities were, deal with them and go home. I really loved the job and because,

I was on my own, I was sort of acting senior engineer unpaid which suited me fine as it meant I was left alone, with only a few mechanical and electrical tradesmen to look after, which suited me fine. I found that just by letting them know what had to be done and trusting them to do it, everything worked out fine. What I also found out, shortly after, was that the hospital secretary, Jim Bell had been the secretary when my sister, Esther had been a nurse there and he remembered her! We had an office just above the reception as you came in the main gate where our secretary, Margaret, worked and, like most secretaries, kept things running smoothly and if I didn't know where to find something, I'd just ask Margaret!

It would be about April when my licence was restored and we had bought a house in Lennoxtown about twenty minutes' drive from Knightswood and within a short period of time I was driving around Glasgow like a native! It was sometime in November, I don't remember the exact date, when I was at work, in the catering manager's office when I felt a funny sort of pain in my chest and just put it down to some kind of indigestion, a throwback to my operation in the RN, thought no more about it until it happened again, a couple of times and I started to wonder. It wasn't till about three in the afternoon, when I was talking to a sales engineer who was trying to sell me something when I totally lost interest in what he was saying and got shot of him, went into the kitchen, came out when I knew he had gone and said to Margaret; "I don't know what's wrong but I don't feel well." She made me sit down and phoned downstairs and asked for a doctor to come round and within minutes, by this time, I was sweating profusely and all the colour had drained from my face (I didn't know that at the time, Margaret told me afterwards). As soon as the doctor had examined me, he ordered an ambulance and when it arrived and had me installed, it had to out the main gate, round the perimeter of the hospital, back in through the back gate and deliver me to the ward where I could be examined thoroughly. After the examination, the doctor told me that I'd suffered a heart attack and would be taken to the coronary care unit in the Western Infirmary and in minutes I was back in the ambulance, lights and sirens going, I think I passed out a couple of times but I can't be sure. The important thing is that, they got me there safely and the next few hours went by in a sort of haze as I had to just lie there and let everybody do their own thing, I don't remember how long I was in coronary care but I know I was kept in for six weeks,(the NHS wasn't under the constraints it is today!) it was during this six week period that I heard that HMS Eagle was being towed up to the breakers yard at Stranraer, I was fast approaching my 46th birthday and the memories came flooding back, all those wasted years and I'm crying again for what might have been! I am not yet at the stage where I am at peace with my past and still have a lot of work to do in that area, but I know that it is coming and reliving these times is quite harrowing, I know it must be done and only I know how cleansing this exercise has been because it is my experience and I am so glad that all those years ago my young sister, Margaret, said that I should write a book and now I'm telling everyone I meet to do the same thing!

I was on sick leave for three months and then I was in on a part time basis for another three months. I still hadn't finished my associate time, it was to be another couple of months before I finally gave in and got back to AA on a full-time basis. It was actually the 20th of August 1979, about 5 weeks short of my 1st meeting of AA 10 years previously. It was a Monday night in Kirkintilloch at the community centre in Hill head and I haven't had a drink of alcohol since that night. There! It's said and I've wanted to say that since I drank that can of shandy all those years ago! By now, it is all change at work and I'm now at Gartnavel Royal which is a large mental hospital which brings back memories of the Ailsa Hospital in Ayr, The good thing about this time is that I'm sober again with no wish to let history repeat itself and determined to do everything in my power to prevent that happening and I'm happy to report that I've been successful, up to today! Today is Sunday, the 9th of July 2017 and I've just arrived back from a retreat in a monastery in Perth with 34 other like-minded AA members. Thing are looking good!

CHAPTER 21

Here we are, into 1980 and I have been moved again, this time to the Western Infirmary, where I had been, just recently, a patient. This is a more modern building although a lot of the old buildings are still here from when my sister was a nurse here in the fifties. A lot of these are being used as office space and the new block, the working hospital. Underground, there are miles of tunnels, carrying all the essentials, like steam, electricity, water and the like. Because of asbestos, quite a few areas have been shut off until specialist teams can remove it, which will be an ongoing task for months! I am still enjoying the job because every day is different with lots of variety, which adds to experience and builds confidence. The other engineers are a good bunch of lads, the only thing I don't like about working for the NHS is the waste, which is so obvious to the front line workers and is unseen by the administration. A case in point was that people making donations didn't seem to be advised about donating sensibly and there was a corridor full of Dialysis machines that couldn't be used because there was no money for maintenance. If the money raised had been given directly to the hospital and they let the staff decide what the greatest priority was, it might have been put to better use!

Anyway the poor old Health Service is still being complained about but it will survive because of the dedicated staff it still has and as always copes and I only hope that we can change this antiquated form of government, which breeds division, which can only be altered if by some strange happenstance, everyone takes Billy Connolly's advice: "Don't vote, you'll only encourage them." What a mess that would be, if they went through all the usual stuff of hiring loads of canvassers, spending millions

136

of pounds when, at the end of polling day, every ballot box was empty. What a movie that would make, especially if it was directed by Billy Connolly! Enough hilarity, for now, I was just giving myself a laugh before I got too serious, politics does that to me and I would love to live in a world without politicians because they prove the point that: "Power corrupts and absolute power corrupts absolutely."

I've decided, after reading that last paragraph, that I am going to skip through the remainder of my working life as I believe in a classless society, but every day I am reminded of the strife that exists between workers and management because I now understand what Malcolm Breen was talking about when I first started! When I was still with Wallacetown Control Systems, we all had to take a turn at being what was called the corresponding member, a glorified shop steward! When it was my turn, the union had set up a weekend seminar in the largest hotel on Rothesay and I was sent along as delegate. At 50p a head, all-expense paid and full board, who could refuse? I'm not going to name the trade union involved, but Neil Kinnock was the sponsored MP! There were workshops covering all sorts of situations but the one that got my attention was: "How to disrupt management". I lost interest at that point and just got drunk for the rest of the weekend.

The last job I had there was as a result of the Senior Engineer at the time having a nervous breakdown while supervising the installation of a building management system and I was asked to take over. I jumped at the chance because of my experience with that primitive computer on HMS Delight and the more up to date one on MV Cape Leeuwin. It was a very complex system and the hardest part was to create a system to identify every component that tied them to the particular function and to alter every drawing accordingly. It was a long and painstaking job, but I thoroughly enjoyed it, especially when it was up and running smoothly. I had various jobs after that until early 1985 when Alan Grey, the District Engineer, who had employed me, asked to see me. Over the last couple of winters, I had been having angina attacks and my doctor immediately put me on the sick, sometimes for a month or longer! Alan said that he knew me well enough and was suggesting that maybe I should consider taking early retirement on health grounds because if I carried on, the job could kill me! I asked him if I could think about it and he said to take my time, it took me about 20 minutes to think about it and I got back to him to tell him that I agreed. I was 52 years old and, having started work with a horse and cart at the age of 12, I decided that I had done my forty years and I had earned my pension time. It was actually the end of November when all the documentation was finalised and I had turned 52, which actually helped because a retirement on health grounds, earned twice the years' service, which meant that I was entitled to 17 years' service. The lump sum allowed us to clear the mortgage and I was reminded of when I retired from the navy on health grounds, I was offered a lump sum of £120 or a weekly payment of 26 old shillings a week! Fortunately, Sheila had the foresight and talked me into accepting the latter, she probably guessed what would have happened to the lump sum!

By this time Alex had been in the Royal Navy since 1975 and was serving in the submarine service and was lucky enough to have served on one of the last remaining diesel boats, Porpoise. I think he'd got the bug after Sheila and he had spent a weekend aboard the Baron Cawdor when we were in Glasgow. He was insistent that he was never going to get married, which meant that we had the freedom to choose whatever we wanted to do with our retirement. We had put a deposit down on a house for him, a one bedroom end terrace, and told him on his next leave. I remember with great clarity, the moment this sense of freedom hit me, it was on a Friday afternoon and we were on our way to an AA convention in Callander. To get to Callander from Lennoxtown, the shortest route was over the Campsie Fells, it was a beautiful afternoon and the view of the mountains in the distance was stunning. It was at this moment, I thought I could see our future, which was more like a spiritual experience than a thought and I just had to share it with Sheila!

When we got home, we started making plans, we both agreed that there was nothing to keep us here and it was just a simple case of deciding where to relocate to and I was happy to leave it up to Sheila, after all, she had certainly earned the right. She was still teaching primary in Kirkintilloch, I told her that if we moved she would have to give up and that she would be retired as well! At long last, I was in a position to let her lean on me as the song goes! What a pity it had taken such a long time! I mentioned earlier about Jim's hobby, fly fishing, while he was training for the prison service in Manchester, he had found this spot in North Wales called Criccieth where he spent most weekends and he never stopped talking about it. My sister, Esther, and her husband, Jim, had a caravan and they'd got into the habit of spending their holidays there, and invited us down one summer. We agreed and I was very pleasantly surprised by the countryside and house prices, so we spent a lot of the time looking, but not finding! The couple who owned the site, John and Margaret Bean, had bought it from the farmer who was there when Jim had found it.

John and his brother were what is known as speculative builders and Margaret kept telling us about the two bungalows they were building in Rhoslan, a hamlet about 2 miles from Criccieth. For some reason or other, I don't know why, we hadn't even thought about looking at them, but on the Sunday before we left for home, I suggested to Sheila that we take a look and she agreed and John took us to have a look. I don't know why, but I had imagined them as being a work in progress and was surprised to find that one was already occupied by a couple from Manchester originally, but who had spent years holidaying there. They invited us in to have a look round and we were both gobsmacked, especially seeing it furnished, they were identical, 3 bedroomed bungalows with an integral garage, solid walls throughout and roofed with real Welsh slates When I told him what I could afford (what I'd got for the house we'd sold) he told me I'd get central heating as well for that price and I immediately shook his hand and told him he had a deal! The only problem was that we would have to vacate about 5 weeks ahead of the new house being ready, so we rented a holiday cottage in the grounds of what had once been Lloyd George's residence. I had started a course with the Open University earlier and it would have been better to have left it until after the move! There was too much going on and then I had to attend a summer school at Stirling University, The course I was taking was a foundation course in mathematics and this turned out be the place where I'd get the second of the only two bouts of tonsillitis I'd ever had in my life, so far! You'll remember the first time was on my honeymoon!

The good thing about being there during the build time was that we got to have a fair bit of input during the later stages, like picking the kitchen units and having a separate shower cubicle in the bathroom and a cupboard to take up the extra space. All the rooms were of a good size, the lounge and dining room running the full width of the bungalow, with a coal open fire in the lounge, which made it especially cosy during the winter months. We were off the main road, the access was a farm road that just led into a field containing a bronze age burial stone so the most traffic we saw, would be the occasional flock of sheep being moved to new pastures! From this field, I had a clear view of Snowdon, which as I mentioned earlier, became my favourite mountain, the reason being, that there were six different paths to the summit. I had only ever done some hill-walking one time before and that was in 1982, when I joined the hospitals hill-walking club, where we met in the village of Stathyre, left the cars at the hotel, took about three cars to the head of Loch Lubnaig and climbed about 800 steep feet to Glen Ample and walked Northwards, coming down on the South Erne Road and then walked back to the hotel in Strathyre. What I haven't mentioned was that it was lashing with rain the full time and whatever way I was facing, the wind changed direction, just so I got used to it! I loved all 15 miles of it, didn't even stop for the tea break and was wearing Alex's Doc Martin boots into the bargain!

I never did any more hill-walking, until we had moved to Wales, I had been up Snowdon a few times and had also joined the local angling club, I wasn't in the same class as Jim had been but I loved the feeling of being close to nature and I did quite a lot of night fishing for sea trout with varying degrees of success. Night fishing can be quite harrowing in the beginning as your imagination can play all sorts of tricks on you, shadows turning into bears and all sorts of wild animals that aren't even native to this part of the world. And then there are the bats that inhabit all rivers in Britain flying about your head and occasionally getting caught on your hook, a very delicate job of surgery to remove them! One day I said to Sheila that I'd like to do the West Highland Way. This was in 1991 and we went up to Scotland and I can't remember where we stayed but I was all set to start the next morning when she met the wife of a friend of mine who was in the fellowship, Timmy Carr, I told him what I was planning and he said he'd like to join me. I'll relate our adventures there in the next chapter.

CHAPTER 22

We are back in Scotland and I don't remember where Sheila has organised our accommodation but I know we are in Lennoxtown, maybe in Alex's house if he is at sea, I may be wrong but it doesn't really affect the story in any way so it not important, except to say, the adventure started here! I know we set off on a Friday morning and our first day's target was Drymen, Sheila drove us to Milngavie supermarket parking lot, which was the official starting point and we made arrangements to meet them there about five, a night's sleep at home then a lift back in the morning to pick up where we left off. The walk from Milngavie to Drymen was pretty straight forward but we were diverted around Conic Hill because of the lambing. We were walking past familiar places because we were still fairly close to home, like the Cherry Tree in close to the old railway walkway, where we had dined fairly regularly before we moved, across Murdock Park, across Stockiemuir road and into an area, that has been famous for the people of Glasgow to build their huts to spend all their weekends there during the thirties. The strange thing was, most of them were still there, probably occupied by the same families or their descendants!

This was a nice gentle introduction to the walk and the sun shone all day, we didn't know it then but we only had a short period of 15 minutes of rain when we were leaving Kinlochleven later in the week! Please remember that this took place in 1991 and my memory could be bit sketchy and some parts may have been moved geographically but if they are mentioned, they are there and Timmy and I trod them! The next day's walk took us from Drymen to Balmaha on the Eastern shore of Loch Lomond, slightly longer but pretty much the same sort of terrain. We were now on our own; I reckon the worst part of the walk was in front of us for the next two days. I'm sharing this from behind the event, instead of prior to it, believe me, it was tough! We had a stop between here and the top of the loch at Rowardennan, a beautiful old country house, converted into a youth hostel, great accommodation and good food. After a good night sleep and breakfast, we set off again past Inversnaid, where the only road on the East side of the loch ends up at the Inversnaid Hotel! By this time, my legs were starting to pain me, my feet were all right because I treat them with Vaseline and sheep's wool, picked off the fence, and wrapped round my toes. This is especially good as the lanolin hasn't been washed out and combined with the Vaseline is a sure cure for blisters! When I talked about the rain a moment ago, I wasn't lying, I just forgot about our next night's accommodation! It was in a caravan behind the house where we had booked B&B and that was the only room left, don't get me wrong, it was comfortable enough, it just poured all night and didn't allow us much sleep before we turned in that night, we visited the famous Drover's Inn, so called because Loch Lomond has been a public right of way for centuries and was on the old drovers road. Inside you are met by a huge stuffed grizzly bear which stands about eight feet tall and the waiters look about the same, only they are wearing kilts! It is standing room only and if you want to eat, the tiny dining room is usually full and you have to eat standing up!

After a fitful night's sleep because of the rain, a hearty breakfast soon got us ready for the day ahead, the rain had stopped and the sun was already out, we set off up Glen Falloch towards Inverarnan where we intended to stop for lunch. When we got there and I was sitting on the grass, enjoying a Mars bar, when a sheep nudged my shoulder and wouldn't stop nudging until I gave her a bite of the Mars bar, I think I made a friend for life and had trouble getting her to stop following me and get back to her mates!

Our next night was booked for Crianlarich but we were going to be there about 11am and we decide to carry on to Tyndrum. We had booked ahead at Rowardennan, where we'd met a young couple who were on their honeymoon. We met them when we got to Crianlarich, so gave them our rooms as a wedding present!

Arriving at Tyndrum, we found a brand new hostel with private rooms, laundry facilities and a restaurant, quite a pleasant surprise after the caravan last night! The other thing that this place is famous for is the Green Welly Shop, which attracts visitors from all over the world. Just past the Green Welly Shop, the road forks, the left hand continuing the A85 towards Oban and the right, the A82 towards Fort William, which is the one we shall be following. Our next stop will be at Bridge of Orchy for lunch, there is a hotel there where we can eat if we need to. We only stopped for a short break, a cup of coffee and pressed on, the ache in my legs has gone and I'm really into this trekking business, back pack and all! We are climbing steadily from here towards the Black Mount, where we start a fairly long descent towards the A82 which we have to cross and head towards the Kings House Hotel which is our next stop. They have a hostel there, which is separate to the hotel but breakfast in the hotel can be included at a cost, but it is well worth it, the menu is unbelievable and the service is fantastic! After such a hearty breakfast, it was just as well l that we had about a couple of miles on the flat before tackling the dreaded Devil's Staircase, there was a bit of a plateau her when a low flying jet frightened the life out of us! The RAF use this as a practice ground for low-level instrument flying with no warning as the plane has passed before the sound catches up! Once we clear the Devil's Staircase the views are stunning, looking down on Loch Leven, the village itself and the Mamore Forest and hills beyond. On the way down we are walking alongside some huge, what I imagine are, water pipes. Why they are there, I don't know but I assume they are something to do with the huge aluminium plant that is at the bottom of the hill. We are about halfway down when I spotted some pieces of paper, on investigation, I saw that they were business cards for a B&B in the village. My immediate reaction was to think that if he or she was prepared to climb this far up, they deserved the business! As soon as we reached the village, I made the phone call and the man who had left the cards came and picked us up and took us to our digs for the night. He lived on his own and as far as I could make out he ran the business by himself and did a very good job, the place was very clean and the food was excellent. The next morning, shortly after we started, the rain came, just a shower for about 15 minutes and the rest of the day clear and sunny! There was a bit of a climb through part of Mamore forest until we reached what is known in Gaelic as Allt na Lairige Moire, a veritable wind tunnel, which even the sun was no match for and we had to break out the heavy gear for the first time on the trip! We were now on the home stretch and with Ben Nevis on our right, we walked through Glen Nevis towards the youth hostel which was the official finish line. I had this terrible mixed feeling of jubilation that I had done it and sorrow that it had ended! We didn't let it end there, another 5 miles into the town and we had rounded it to a good 100 miles. That night there was an AA meeting in the hospital, we went there and told them that we had walked from Glasgow to get there! It had taken us just six days to complete, which made me feel quite proud of myself, until a nephew, a son of my sister Esther, Kenneth Lorimer, ran it in 19 hours!

The good thing about this experience was that it had given me a taste for trekking and I wanted to do more and so did Timmy. So we made a promise to each other that the next one would be the Southern Upland Way, across 212 miles of some of the most varied and beautiful landscapes in Scotland. It was to be another two years before we managed it. I won't go into another step by step account because reading about it is not the same as doing it. Suffice to say that it had to end half way through because I'd torn my Achilles tendon. Timmy just had a new grandson and was missing him so was quite pleased to give up. The other things he didn't like were washing his face in the burn and being woken up in the middle of the night, just because there was a mouse in his sleeping bag! I don't think he ever did another trek! All my remaining treks were done with a friend in North Wales, who had also been in the RN and was an experienced hill walker.

It was also during my hill-walking that I discovered the other place where I was touched by Eternity and I have only found two, so the chances of finding another at my time of life are pretty remote! The other place was on a ship in the middle of an ocean, standing alone on the fore deck where all that can be seen is sea and sky. I am thinking I am alone, when you become aware of something and there, swimming alongside is a giant turtle, heading towards the Galapagos Islands just to lay some eggs, using one flipper at a time, not in a great hurry, because time has no meaning for her! Another time, while I was on the after deck, I watched a killer whale keeping station of the port quarter for about two hours, and the most wonderful experience that can only be found in the Southern Hemisphere is to watch the Albatross as it skims the waves with only inches to spare and maybe only flapping its wings once every 15 minutes or so. It is at these times when we think we are alone that nature lets us know that it is still there and always has been. This is why I am writing this history of my experiences, because I am so grateful to have survived life, both the good times and especially the bad, in order to pass it on and if only one person benefits from my experience, then my living has not been in vain!

CHAPTER 23

So, here we are, into the nineties and all is well with the house and garden, although the garden took a bit of effort, remember that it stood fallow for over 2,000 years before I took it on. It was full of boulders and rocks that required crowbars and pickaxes to remove, plus the muscles of some of the younger members of the neighbours! I had gone into the forest before we left Scotland and purloined three Rowan tree saplings and planted them just inside the gate so that we could call the house The Rowans. Unfortunately, one of them died and I had to purchase a Welsh one from John's brother who had a nursery. The place is now looking good and lived in, with a hedge between our neighbours on the left and shrubs surrounding the fuel tank in the corner. I've converted one of the bedrooms into a study, where I've installed my computer equipment and books, Sheila has a part time job in a charity shop which she really enjoys, so we are now quite settled into our new lives and the only thing that is different is that Alex has a girlfriend in Lennoxtown and is talking about marriage. So much for us thinking there was nothing to hold us back as Alex was convinced he was never going to get married!

There is a strange coincidence that is connected to how I made contact with AA in Wales and goes back to the time when we were on the camp site with Jim and Esther when we first saw the house. We didn't have mobile phones then but there was an AA box on the road just outside the site, as I was a member of both I used their phone to contact the other AA and was given a number to ring. It turned out to be John from Nefyn who was a member and took me to my first meeting in Wales. John and I are still friends and I last saw him and his wife in

Dumfries a couple of years ago at a convention. After that first phone call, the phone box was removed! After we had got settled into the house, John and I decided to open a meeting in Pwllheli, about midway between us geographically, as the only other meeting near us was in Porthmadog. The first time I went there I was disgusted to find that there were absolutely no signs that this was an AA meeting and was held in a children's classroom. When I asked why they were in such an uncomfortable venue, I was told that a couple of local business men, who were afraid of their anonymity, persuaded the group to move out of an anonymous building in the main street, so that they wouldn't be seen going in there! When I asked where they were now, I was told they were both back on the drink! My answer to that was: "I know we are anonymous but we don't have to be invisible!" The other thing I didn't like about that meeting was that they never talked about recovery, which is the sole purpose of an AA group!

John and I found premises to rent in Pwllheli on a Monday night and called it The Three Legacies Group, to remind ourselves of our primary purpose, which was to help the still suffering alcoholic, the three legacies being, Unity, Recovery and Service. It took a few weeks to take off but it soon became popular as Pwllheli was a very popular holiday destination for people from the likes of Liverpool and Manchester and alcoholics on holiday usually carry a "Where to Find", the directory of meetings with contact numbers and as soon as our group was included, it became even busier! This terrible disease is acknowledged by no less an authority than the World Health Organisation as the 3rd biggest killer, and for every active alcoholic, there are at least 4 or 5 people, directly affected! When I studied the history of Alcoholics Anonymous, I found that it came into being on the 10th of June 1935, when Bill Wilson met Dr. Bob Smith and shared his experience with him, Dr. Bob got sober and together they carried the message to AA member number 3. The rest is history and, if you remember me telling you about my very first resentment, this would be about the time when Bill met Dr. Bob and I still tell people that Bill wrote the Big Book, because he knew I was coming!

I was still thoroughly enjoying life, but there was a constant little niggle bothering me. It was a feeling of inadequacy that I hadn't yet dealt with, what had caused me to go back on the drink. I was, at this time very active in the service side of AA, being the group service representative to intergroup and Intergroup's representative to Region and this niggle was niggling me more here! It was to be removed shortly but in a manner least expected! A couple of years previously, I had brought a young Irishman from Porthmadog into the fellowship and he and a friend had heard about a couple of Americans who had been invited over to do a series of Big Book seminars and decided to go and hear them. After they got back, I noticed a terrific difference in them, especially the Irishman. When I asked them about what they were like, they told me how simple they made things seem and I made a decision that, as soon as possible, I would attend one of their seminars. In the meantime, I asked John if he would show me the programme as they had explained it to him. He agreed and we made arrangements that we'd meet at his house one afternoon, I can't remember what day it was, I should because the result had such a profound effect on the rest of my life. When it came to sharing my darkest secrets, it turned out that the secret he couldn't share was exactly the same one I had hidden for all those years! The next step asked me to take myself to a place of comfort and reflect on these five proposals, I took myself home and got settled into my favourite chair and was extremely surprised to find that I was entirely ready to have God remove all my defects of character! On reflection, I decided that why this had not happened previously was because I had not done step five properly and I was afraid of what I might turn into without my defects. This is what I meant about this having a profound effect on my life, I was no longer afraid! All I had done was to do what I should have done years ago then go home, sit on my bum, and let things happen! I still have a slight sense of inadequacy, but I am happy with the fact that I still have flaws. The programme tells us that we claim spiritual progress rather than spiritual perfection and if, as I believe it is, spiritual perfection is a finite spot in space, then, by daily progress, I am closing the distance and just maybe, with my last gasp, the gap will be nil!

It would be about this time that I was nominated as a Conference Delegate to York for the annual conference, I remember the feeling as I drove home from the Regional meeting, knowing that I was going to conference to represent my group in Pwllheli, a very humbling experience! Every region sends six delegates, one to sit on one of the six committees. I was selected to sit on committee number six, which dealt with all questions relating to literature. Our intergroup belonged to Number One Region, which covered the whole of the Northwest of England and North Wales.

Anyway, enough of that, it was just another unnecessary digression which interrupted my chain of thought and, whenever that happens, I'm left with a decision to make, delete it or leave it in. In this case, I don't have to let you know my decision! I'll have to work harder on my humility!

Even though I'm now living a very healthy regime, non-smoker, non-drinker, hill walker and angler, I was quite surprised when my doctor wanted me to have some checks done on my heart. I was admitted to Gwynedd general hospital in Bangor. I'd been having the odd angina attack, but had the medication to deal with it, so it wasn't the problem it had been in the past. Because the waiting list for angiograms was so long, they decided to send me to Cardiff, they must have thought it urgent. As it turned out, I believe it was all the extra medication I was on that made me have a funny turn while waiting to be admitted and they took me straight to the ward and put me to bed. After the angiogram, I was told that only one artery was slightly blocked and nothing to worry about. I went back home, stopped taking the medicines that I knew I didn't need and was fine for the next eight years! One of the things that I got into the habit of was to get Sheila to drop me off at a beautiful little spot called Cwm Bwchan. It was at the end of a dead end road with nothing but a farm and surrounded by a ring of hills surrounding a lake. I'd pitch my tent and stay for a couple of nights just watching the wild goats, fascinated by their sure-footedness! What peace!

My mate, Paul Brown, and I covered a lot of ground in the next couple of years, the first being the western half of Wainwright's walk across England, we drove to Kendal in the Lake District, left our car with a mate who lived there, who then drove us to St. Bees Head and left us to get on with it! He picked us up, six days later at Keld, on the other side of the Pennines, took us back to Kendal where we retrieved the car and headed back to Wales! I also managed to get the Southern Upland Way completed by first doing the eastern half with Paul, then later in the year, the western half which was my second time, without the torn Achilles tendon! The other important one was the Fifteen Peaks in North Wales, done in July with absolutely brilliant weather, not a cloud in the sky, with the views from every peak stunning! The other thing of note that happened that year, in fact, there were two things in fairly rapid succession that I tend to remember them as one. They were both to do with my fly fishing, the first one afternoon when I was fishing the Dwyfor and a sea trout about 8 pounds took my fly, went deep and stayed there. My landing net was slung over my shoulder and, while I was trying to get it over my head, my hat fell off, I tried to pick it up and my glasses fell off, this was the moment that the fish decided to surface and escape! I dreamt of that fish for days! The other incident happened on a Saturday afternoon on the same river but farther upstream, I had just cast across to just behind a bush on the opposite bank, when this monster of a fish took me and headed downstream without stopping, taking my tackle with him! I thought that was the end of it, till next morning when I was just walking up the bank to start fishing, when I saw this fish lying at the side, obviously dead. I could hardly believe my eyes when I saw the size of it and assumed that it must have been this fish that I'd had on the previous day, even if only for a second or two! I had some bright yellow waterproof leggings in the boot, so I retrieved the fish from the river, slid it inside one of the legs, dumped it in the boot and drove home. When I arrived and parked in our drive, I noticed that Gordon was working in his garden, keeping a straight face I asked him if I could borrow his wheel barrow. When he asked what for I told him I needed it to get this fish into the garage! When I told him that I wasn't joking and showed him what was in the boot, he was amazed, even more so when I told him that I was only using 4 pound tackle. When I got it into the garage and measured it, it was 43 inches long and when I tried to weigh it with my spring balance, its jaw broke! It weighed in at just over 33 pounds. I had contacted the secretary of the angling club and told him the story, he came up and couldn't decide whether it was a salmon or sea trout or even a hybrid. He took it away and sent some scales off to a laboratory, but even they weren't sure. If it was a sea trout, it would have broken the British record and I had to tell them that I had found it in a state of deadness!

CHAPTER 24

Here we are, well into the nineties, I've finished my three years at conference, I thoroughly enjoyed the experience but am glad it's behind me. It means that I can concentrate on getting involved in life outside AA, not that I am ignoring the fellowship, just that I am not so heavily involved in service. I am still an active member of my home group and attend the occasional convention. It is a way of life that I have taken on in order to maintain and accept my responsibilities towards my family and society. My health has steadied up and I am not having any serious problems, whenever I'm asked what keeps me so healthy, I tell whoever is asking that I've had all the bad bits removed with only the working bits left!

Maybe I've been spared all these years so that I can finish this book, I maybe have mentioned this earlier, but I do think sometimes, that is what Lord Kitchener wanted me for, but then I think, why would somebody, who has already passed away, tell a four year old child to stick around for eighty years to write a book? Who knows, stranger things are happening every day! Have I mentioned lately my eternal optimism? It just dawned on me that I hadn't and I wonder why, is it because I've been granted the serenity to accept the things I cannot change and I have reached a point in my life where my will and my life are in the hands of a far greater power than I could ever be where I've reached, what I spoke about in the prologue, full circle, back to the safety of the spiritual womb and total dependence! Please excuse the meanderings, it is again the result of a digression! I do know why I am doing this and I think I owe the reader an explanation, the reason is very simple, I am coming to the point in my life where my whole reason for being is removed, I'm talking about

153

the illness and death of my soulmate and life partner, Sheila. Maybe I was delaying reliving the experience because I knew it would be harrowing but it has to be done as this book wouldn't be complete without this retelling!

Sheila had been having problems with her breathing, she was a long time asthma sufferer and had to attend hospital for heart and a lung check-up. When the specialist examined her he said her heart and lungs were fine, but she had cancer of the pancreas and because of where it was, it was inoperable. I'm almost certain that the date he told us this was the 1st of July 1996.I remember the first words she said to me was: "Iain, this isn't fair on you" and I asked her what she meant and she said about me losing my mother and brother so young, and all I could say was that maybe it was to prepare me for this! Again I'm asking myself, why Sheila and not me because she was the one who had put up with all the trouble I had caused over the years. Anyway, I hope that I have conveyed just how much I loved Sheila and that instinct when I first met her and asked her to marry me after four days was the best thing I ever did in my life. The day I took her home from the hospital was the start of what I still tell people was the best seven months of my life. Please believe me when I say this because I was given the chance to really make amends for all the suffering I had caused her over the years, I told her I loved her every day and I was nursing the young nurse I had met all those years ago in Brighton and we were walking the South Downs again. I bought a lot of the essential oils and massaged her arms and legs every day. This was her time, and I made sure her every wish was carried out as far as I could. Her main wish was that she wouldn't have to go back into hospital and she never did, except for a few days shortly after the diagnosis for pain management.

Alex was well married, with two children, Craig and Aillie, 7 and 5, they were down whenever they could during this time and Sheila was always delighted to see

154

them. I was just so sad that they were going to lose their gran while they were still so young, especially as Elaine's mother had died just before Craig was born. There was one thing that I couldn't understand and that was her lifelong friend and bridesmaid, Dorothy, should not be allowed to visit her. I found this hard to explain whenever Dorothy phone to ask after Sheila because she would probably feel very hurt when I insisted that this was Sheila's wish and I was only the messenger! She was very persistent and one day I answered the phone to hear that she was in a phone box, just a couple of hundred yards away, I don't know whether Sheila had changed her mind or not but I was so angry, that Dorothy had driven all the way from Liverpool against Sheila's wishes, that I just told her to turn back and return to Liverpool! I felt terrible but Sheila must have had her reasons and that was what I was respecting but still angry that Dorothy couldn't do the same! I learned a lot about people and how kind they could be in situations like this but also, extremely unthinking, one of our neighbours stopped me one day when I was on my way to the chemist to pick up Sheila's prescription and insisted that I let her help. I thanked her very much for her offer and told her that we had all the help that we needed but that if there was anything I would ask. She then said that she didn't want to interfere and I had to interrupt her to tell her that she was interfering because I was on the way to pick up a prescription and she was holding me up! She took off in a huff! We really did have all the help we could hope for from the local surgery staff, MacMillan and Marie Curie nurses and friends who would stay over so that I could get a sleep. Then there were the days when I might be out in the car for something or other and it would suddenly hit me, that what was happening was real and I found myself sobbing desperately. The other thing I came to realise over time was how privileged we are to be allowed to share someone's last moments, I'll never forget the night Sheila died, she had been in a coma for over a week, Alex was with me in the lounge when the nurse came through and said: " I think it's time you came through". Alex stayed where he was and I went through on my own and held her in my arms till she passed out of my life. I went through to the lounge to let Alex know that it was all over and I thought of that moment in the train all those years ago when we were taking him home for the first time! The nurse came through and asked if I wanted her to take her wedding ring off, without thinking, I said: "No, I put it on, I'll take it off." I'm looking at it now, on my little finger of my right hand, kept in place by my AA ring. If you want to know what I was thinking at this time, go back to the prologue, this was written on the day of Sheila's funeral. Come the 5th of February, next year, it will be 21 years since that day and I've just spent the last five minutes sobbing my heart out reliving those moments! The funeral went very well, with lots of friends from all over. Sheila was a lot like my mother, she was very popular and made friends easily and like my mother, a lifelong knitter, maybe that was what had attracted me to her in the first place, she had knitted the little beret she was wearing the first day I saw her! She is buried in a beautiful place overlooking Cardigan Bay and if Glasgow University doesn't accept my body for science, I shall be laid to rest beside her, when my time comes.

A neighbour of ours in Lennoxtown had died a few days after Sheila and her funeral was on the 7th, so I decided to travel up on the Thursday to attend and pay our respects. All the way up, I had a terrible feeling that I shouldn't have left and as soon as the funeral was over on the Friday, I set off back home and didn't stop. I had this feeling of urgency that I couldn't explain but seemed to be driving me. On the M6, a few miles north of the M54, where I had to turn off for Wales, the sky turned very dark and the heavens opened up with torrential rain. A soon as I crossed the border into Wales, the rain stopped and the sky turned blue with a perfect half circle of a rainbow, every colour bright and I felt fine. If you have an explanation of what I had just witnessed and why, I really don't need to know, it was enough for me to have experienced this and to know that I was where I was supposed to be! It was strange going back to an empty house and I spent the next few months spending a few weeks here and there in Scotland. My friend from Troon, Iain Hunter had a holiday chalet near Crianlarich which he let me borrow for two weeks, he spent the first week with me and then left me on my own for a week. Shortly after I rented a chalet between Comrie and Crieff for a month and really enjoyed the time on my own. I don't suppose that I spent too much time in Wales, during that first year, I spent quite a bit of time in various places around Elgin, in the north east of Scotland, where I felt a curious affinity, on researching the Clan McMillan's history, I discovered we were descended from a Pictish tribe and the Gaelic name translated to son of the tonsured one, obviously priests. Maybe this accounted for the strange affinity I felt towards the area!

Ever since I read a book by Deepak Chopra called "The Seven Laws For Spiritual Success" and going down to hear a lecture of his in Manchester, I've been fascinated by Quantum Physics and try to keep up to date with what is happening. I've learned how to keep it simple since I met that theoretical physicist in the electrical school in HMS Collingwood all those years ago, and that is, keep it simple before it gets too complex to understand! All I need to know about Quantum Physics is that the whole universe is made up of minute particles of information and energy which are all interconnected and communicating with each other. Maybe you are asking yourself: "Why does he believe this?" I believe in this theory because of people like Stephen Hawking, who has defied the laws of nature by surviving a disease that should have killed him before the age of thirty and said of himself that it was no coincidence that he chose theoretical physics as a career! And Einstein, who built his theory on an assumption and, using logic, proved it! Logic, like hindsight, is an exact science, and because I have a simple mind, it is easier to trust people like these, who have done all the hard work, than to ask them to prove it! Trust is one of those words that, when you hear it, makes you wonder why are they asking, especially if they don't know you? My way of dealing with this sort of situation is to treat trust like faith, if I know someone whom I trust, I have faith in them. If I don't know someone, how can I trust them?

CHAPTER 25

Here we are, approaching the end of the nineties and I'm still here, although not quite as healthy as when I last spoke to you! I've had another angiogram and been told that I need a triple bypass, it will be carried out at the Manchester Royal Infirmary in February 1999. It took place on the 2nd of February and everything went well, except for the fact that I had a terrible attack of the hiccups which went on for days. There was one day, my bed was surrounded by the surgical team and nurses involved in my operation and I told them: "It must have cost thousands of pounds to train all of you people, and yet not one of you can cure a dose of hiccups!" The moment passed without comment or suggestion and the day came for my release, and what a day that was. I was ready and waiting from 9am and it was after 5pm when a private hire came with just a driver and no medical person to drive me back to North Wales where I would be admitted to a cottage hospital the other side of Porthmadog. The worst was yet to come, as soon as we set off the driver informed me that he had another pickup from another hospital to deliver to somewhere on the Lynn Peninsula, it turned out to be halfway up a mountain, they were an elderly couple and obviously, he dropped them off first! It was approaching 10pm when I was eventually delivered to my destination, which turned out to be a lovely, old fashioned type cottage hospital that I remember from my childhood. I was to spend a month there recuperating and this more than made up for the journey from Hell to get there!

The previous year, while visiting Elgin, one of the members of AA told me that she had a touring caravan to sell, an 18 footer complete with awning and, after viewing it I had no hesitation in offering her the asking price and arranged to have it towed to a camp site which had at one time been Balquhidder Station. This meant that I had a base in Scotland whenever I needed a break and now was the ideal time!

After my discharge from hospital, I spent a couple of weeks at home, before heading north to the caravan, which by now had all my personal stuff, including my fishing and walking gear as I had used it a couple of times previously. This would be towards the end of March and I felt fully recovered from the operation although the scars were still very obvious but as I wasn't in the habit of going around topless, no one would see them. The other good thing about the surgeons in Manchester was that they used the mammary arteries instead of going into my legs or arms, which made up for their lack of skills in the hiccups department!

I had been up Snowdon since getting home and I was planning to join a charity trek to the Himalayas in August, so I had to start planning and raising money, I did this by printing out sponsorship forms and leaving them in places like the local surgery and shops. I also had an article with a photograph in the local paper. The charity concerned was The Leonard Cheshire Homes and by adding car boot sales, the required amount was soon raised and I was all set to go. I still had a lot to do in the fitness area, remember that I am now approaching 67 and not as young as I used to be, so I am planning to do some climbing while I'm in Scotland. The 2 peaks I have in mind are, Ben More and Ben Lawers, both within the ten highest peaks in Scotland. There are 283 Munros in Scotland and I have now done 3 of them because to reach the peak of Ben Lawers, I was required to reach it via Ben Glass, which is also a Munro (over 3,000 feet) Ben Lawers is the higher of the two and when I neared the summit I had to cross the snow line where I spotted a hare with its winter camouflage, a white coat!

August came and it was time for the big adventure, I got the train from Pwllheli down the Cambrian coast then inland to Wolverhampton where I changed for London, arriving there, I made my way to Heathrow where I met up with another 71 strangers who were to spend the next week together along with the organising team plus interpreters, as we'd be using local guides, who were mostly Russian speaking. We'd be flying into Tashkent in Uzbekistan which is at the western end of the Himalayas and the start of the old Silk Road to China. Tashkent, when we arrived there looked very poor and the hotel we stayed looked as if the furniture had been bought from a charity shop and none of it matched however, the coaches when they arrived to transport us into the foothills were very modern looking and quite luxurious, very different to the transport provided to take us to our first camp site! They were ex Russian military vehicles which had seen better days and the journey from here looked quite perilous, as it turned out to be! We had left the real road with the coaches and were now faced with nothing but dirt tracks, boulders and potholes. The driver of our van must have had aspirations of being a formula one driver, the way he took those bends at speed. However, the way he was driving could only end one way and it did! I don't know what happened but we found ourselves and the van, tilted at a 45-degree angle, hanging over a 400 foot drop. Luckily for us, the van was a left-hand drive and the largest guy in the van was sitting in the passenger seat and immediately got out and held the van until the driver could get all four wheels back on track! You would think that any driver, having gone through such an experience would be a bit more cautious, at least for a couple of hours or so. But not this driver, it seemed like less than half an hour later, I was dozing when I was rudely awakened by a violent movement sideways of the van and I immediately thought of that 400 foot drop when I felt the van rolling and I was preparing for the bump when we hit the bottom. It wasn't to be, all that had happened was that the van had rolled over onto the roof and then rolled back onto her side. The amazing thing was that no one was hurt, except one guy had bumped his head on the door, when I said it was amazing, this was because not one seat was secured to the floor and we also had several cases of bottled water flying all over the place without counting the bodies. All this and we haven't started walking yet! Only another 120 kilometres to go. Apart from that, the rest of the trek went well and we raised in total over £300,000.

Because I had enjoyed this trek so much, I decided to do another one the following year 2000, the first year of the new millennium. This would be in the Namib Desert in Namibia, the oldest desert in the world, and all my fund raising this time would be done from my caravan as a base. I had the rest of the campsite visitors who were regulars and I knew most of them. The other thing I did was to persuade a few of my friends in AA to join me on a sponsored Zip wire across the River Clyde from the top of the Clyde port Crane at Anderson Dock which, coincidentally was erected in 1932, the year of my birth! This turned out to be another fascinating experience and led to further adventures in the future, the wife of the couple who were organising the camps had parents who owned a huge farm on the way to Windhoek and organised that I could stay with there for a week after the trek finished. It only meant altering my flight time home and an extra £5 for insurance! I had a wonderful time both on the trek and especially on the farm as I spent most of my time going out with Ernest on his pickup round his vast farm where there were all sorts of wild game, especially the baboons. He also told me of an apartment they owned in Swakopmund that they would be happy to rent out to me for a modest rent, which I took them up on the following January and February and loved it!

After my holiday and a month at home, I headed for the caravan for a few weeks and to take in the Scottish AA convention in Perth. The caravan has turned out to be one of the best ideas I've had as its position is quite remote, yet central for access to a lot of the places where some of my favourite meetings are. If I had known what was going to happen at the convention and the outcome, I would definitely have changed my mind and stayed home! But, insight is an exact science and I take full responsibility for the next five years, which I am going to gloss over and just stick to my decision and the consequences of making that decision! The convention ran from the Friday through till Sunday lunch time, with meetings and a dance on the Saturday night. Because Saturday night was a formal do, I had my dress kilt outfit on and was sitting right at the end of a table up against the wall. There was an empty seat next to mine and this woman climbed over everyone seated between her and the empty seat and started talking. She told me that she came from Redcar in the north east of England, there was something about her that had me intrigued and we ended up talking till about 1am and arranged to meet for breakfast and that was the start of 6 years of turmoil for me, my only excuse was that in the beginning, she made me very happy. We married in the July of that year and I remember how emotional I felt when I made the wedding vows. I know now that she engineered the engagement and the wedding, as soon as the wedding was over, I started to see the other side of her. This won't take long in the telling, but it felt like an eternity living through it! The marriage lasted five years, it should only have lasted one, but I felt a bit like Michelangelo, I could see the angel in the rock, but I couldn't release her. We moved house 5 times in 5 years because she couldn't settle and eventually I'd had enough, packed all my worldly goods in the back of the car and left. I drove back to Stirling and asked a friend if she could put me up for a couple of days till I could sort myself out. The caravan had gone as well as my savings and I was in debt to the tune of £20,000. I shared a flat with another AA member for a month while I declared myself homeless and I was rehoused in less than three months in sheltered housing just minutes from Stirling Castle and stayed there until seven years ago come November this year. I got all of my finances sorted out while I was there and I'm back to where I should never have left, without fear of people or financial insecurity and absolutely no bitterness towards Margaret! During that five years with Margaret I had to have more surgery, first because I was having a lot of acid reflux, they had to do a bypass in my digestive system because I had no gall bladder, so they redirected the bile, then they had to do another one to fix the surgical hernia the first operation had left me with!

I left Stirling six years ago last November and I'll have been here seven years come this November. The reason for the move was that, if I had to stop driving, it would mean getting a bus into Glasgow, then a bus from Glasgow to here, which would take about an hour and a half. I applied to all the housing associations in the area and was lucky enough to get a flat in another sheltered housing less than ten minutes' walk from Alex's house, where I go round for my breakfast one day every weekend. So, here I am, a long way from there and very happy to be here with my memories and friends, I hope you have enjoyed the journey, I've loved having you with me, and thanks for your company.

Printed in Great Britain
by Amazon